CULT EYEWEAR

CULT EYEWEAR

The World's Enduring Classics

Neil Handley

MERRELL
LONDON · NEW YORK

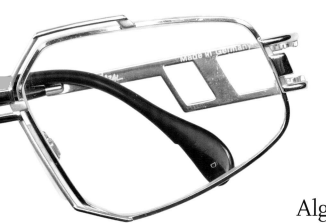

WARNING.

It has come to our notice that Imitation Shell and Coloured Spectacles of several of the designs below illustrated are being displayed and offered for sale which are not of our manufacture.

We hereby give notice, that,—all these being our Registered Designs immediate proceedings will be taken against anybody infringing our rights by offering for sale or displaying any of these patterns that are not of our own manufacture.

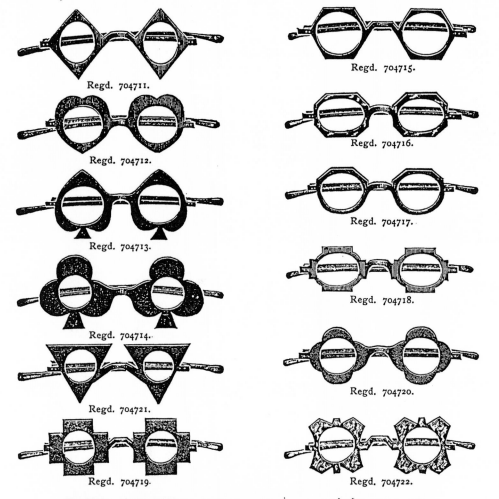

Regd. 704711.

Regd. 704715.

Regd. 704712.

Regd. 704716.

Regd. 704713.

Regd. 704717.

Regd. 704714.

Regd. 704718.

Regd. 704721.

Regd. 704720.

Regd. 704719.

Regd. 704722.

KIRK BROTHERS
WHOLESALE & MANUFACTURING OPTICIANS
36. GRAY'S INN ROAD, LONDON, W.C.1

Telephones HOLBORN { 1620 4582   Telegrams KIRBROREX, HOLB. LONDON.

An Illustrated List of above Designs suitable for a Showcard can be had on application.

Introduction

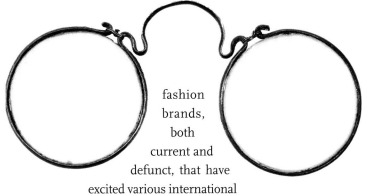

This is the type of book that, not so long ago, would have annoyed many opticians. It is not a history of a benevolent functional device, from the reading stones of the first millennium through to the progressive lenses of the third. It is not an account of how clear sight was restored to the visually impaired, of headaches relieved, working lives extended or obstacles to learning removed. It is not about vision aids as such but rather about spectacle frames, those practical structures for supporting corrective or protective lenses in front of the eyes (although it hasn't always been necessary to wear a glazed frame in order to initiate or follow an eyewear fashion trend). More specifically, this book offers a deliberate and inevitably somewhat personal selection from the myriad of designer fashion brands, both current and defunct, that have excited various international markets over the past century. They are the so-called 'cult' brands, that is to say, those brands that have built up a distinct following, whether mass or niche, whether lasting or ephemeral. Some of the brands have enjoyed cult status throughout their existence; others have had it only to lose it, or sometimes, after an interval of time, regain past glories. Some of these brands have sought to appeal to the avant-garde, while others were surprised, maybe even embarrassed, by the commercial reaction they received from the buying public.

A sixteenth- or seventeenth-century frame made in Nuremberg, Bavaria, of a simple one-piece wire construction that allowed mass production. Although oval rims have been traced back to 1510, until the nineteenth century most rims remained round.

OPPOSITE
A Kirk Brothers advertisement from 1924.

7

Goldoni-type spectacles from Venice *c.* 1790, missing their original sewn-on silk 'shades'. Named after Carlo Goldoni, master of the Commedia dell'Arte, spectacles of this type were arguably the first to increase their market significantly on account of their association with a celebrity.

St Jerome, patron saint of spectacle makers, is not wearing his glasses in this copy of a fifteenth-century Florentine fresco, but they are hanging from the side of his writing desk, ready for use as required.

Cult eyewear is a particular type of fashion; not every spectacle wearer can carry it off – and talking of carrying things off, a major criterion for inclusion in this book was whether the brand featured in the regular listings that have appeared in the professional press of frames stolen from optical practices. A lesser consideration was whether the brand has ever attracted celebrity adherents. Here we must be careful. Lists of famous wearers are not enough, for few notable figures have confined themselves to just one brand or even to just one brand at a time. Although late eighteenth-century Venetian citizens flocked to emulate the horn-rimmed 'shades' (spectacles with attached awning-like silk fabric) of the dramatist Carlo Goldoni, the celebrity spectacle wearer is not always admired. When Johnny Depp visited the American Library in Paris to research his role in the film *Chocolat* (2000) wearing nearly opaque coin-sized sunglasses, the librarian who handed him membership details reportedly said, 'And take off those glasses. They annoy me.'

Even the dramatis personae who present the cult eyewear to us for our delight and delectation have been known to go off message, sometimes at the most inconvenient of times. Sophia Loren, who had her own eponymous brand of spectacles out at the time, caused embarrassment to her commercial licensees in the mid-1980s when she was photographed at a trade show trying on glasses at the Michael Selcott stand. Gianni Versace, who first issued his own line in 1978, was apparently wearing spectacles by Cutler and Gross (p. 113) when he was shot dead in 1997.

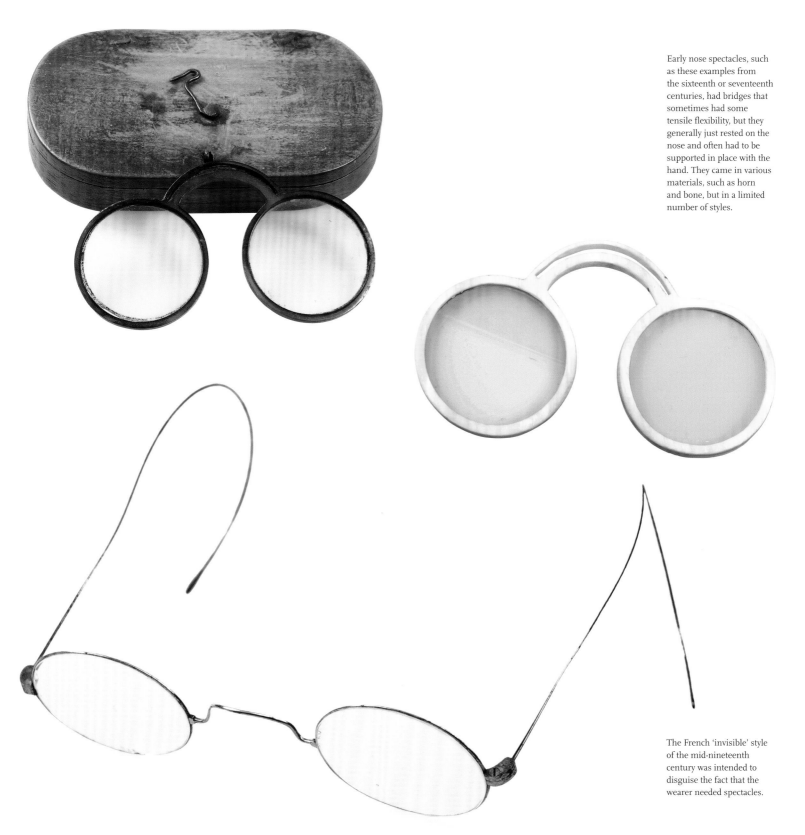

Early nose spectacles, such as these examples from the sixteenth or seventeenth centuries, had bridges that sometimes had some tensile flexibility, but they generally just rested on the nose and often had to be supported in place with the hand. They came in various materials, such as horn and bone, but in a limited number of styles.

The French 'invisible' style of the mid-nineteenth century was intended to disguise the fact that the wearer needed spectacles.

'Nuremberg Masterpiece' spectacles made in 1663 by Melchior Schelkle, designed less for wear than to demonstrate his prowess. The carved filigree pattern features thirty-nine small hearts along the top of the rim and a further fourteen below, clover motifs and the letter Y (sideways on each side of the horizontal lines between the hearts and the clovers), plus a spiral on each side of the nose.

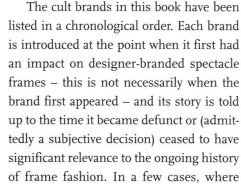

The cult brands in this book have been listed in a chronological order. Each brand is introduced at the point when it first had an impact on designer-branded spectacle frames – this is not necessarily when the brand first appeared – and its story is told up to the time it became defunct or (admittedly a subjective decision) ceased to have significant relevance to the ongoing history of frame fashion. In a few cases, where they emerged from the same company stable, brands have been grouped together; notably, the brands associated with Wilhelm Anger (such as Viennaline/Serge Kirchhofer; p. 87) and Frank Wiseman (such as Algha/Mary Quant/Savile Row; p. 55).

For similar reasons of practicality, I have opted to recount the full history of a brand in a single place, even when the brand changed ownership (for example Ray-Ban; p. 67), or when the brand name itself was modified (as in the case of Carrera/Carrera Porsche Design/Porsche Design; p. 77).

The rise of cult brands

For some optometrists and, indeed, some dispensing opticians, it was all too much to see their beloved medical appliances – spectacles that were often very well made and carefully selected, and that might last a lifetime – turning into items of consumer desire and whim, to be cast aside for the next style or even just a change of colour. They campaigned against creeping commercialism, and in Britain the display of prices in the window of a practice was prohibited until 1985. In today's world of two-for-one offers and even 'free' eye examinations it is easy to see how the pendulum has swung so far that even those who pushed for change may take pause for thought, as the business model of the independent high-street optometrist has perhaps started to be called into question.

This book describes the actions of some of those 'shopticians' who wanted to break out of what they regarded as professional stuffiness, who wanted to offer the public something different, something exciting and noticeable. One could suggest that they identified correctly which way the wind was blowing or, alternatively, that the outcome would not have been the same without their input. Many of them were certainly isolated in their day, being shunned and admired in perhaps equal measure by their peer group. Although devotees of a cult will raise its founders to positions of the highest exaltation, this book is not intended to elevate them any higher, but merely to document their contribution, for better or for worse, to the frames business we know today.

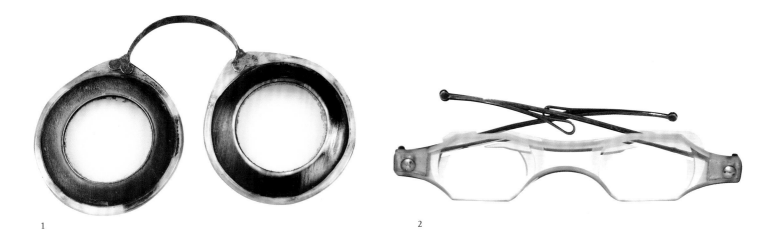

1

3

4

1
One of the immensely
popular 'Visual Glasses'
by Benjamin Martin of
London, *c.* 1770, which
featured an inner rim
of horn or shell.

2
One of the earliest rimless
styles was the *Waldsteinsche
Brillen*, a one-piece front
introduced in the mid-
nineteenth century by
Jacob Waldstein of Vienna.
The spectacles were
popularly known as
'intelligence glasses'.

3
Display spectacles by
pioneering British frame
designer Stanley Unger,
c. 1950, with printed
decoration echoing a
Nuremberg Masterpiece.

4
Early eighteenth-century
ornamental spectacles in
'German silver' (nickel
silver) with inlaid wood case.

José Buzo Caceres, *Portrait of a Gentleman*, 1832. This Spanish portrait is unusual not only for showing in such precise detail an example of D-spectacles (a new style at the time), but also for the fact that the eyes of the sitter are not visible. The spectacles might possibly conceal ocular disease.

A retail head displaying Perivist lenses by the German firm Zeiss, 1936. At the time Zeiss made high-quality, popular frames, but its marketing firmly emphasized the lenses.

The *Oxford English Dictionary* (OED) defines the adjective 'cult' as 'designating cultural phenomena with a strong, often enduring appeal to a relatively small audience'. This audience is often on the fringes, away from the mainstream, and over time this can give rise to connotations of an exclusive cachet. Yet cult followings can also grow – sometimes rapidly – as the desirability of a product increases and awareness of its existence rises. It is possible to identify some historic antecedents to the cult eyewear of modern times.

Incidentally, the first OED-verified use of the word 'eyewear' dates from an advertisement in the *Glasgow Herald* in 1926. While earlier uses probably remain to be discovered, the late coining of the word possibly reflects an enduring folk memory that early spectacles were generally hand-held, or at least supported in front of the face with the fingers, and that for centuries they were used only intermittently for specific tasks and put away again. As such, in their origins, they were not 'eyewear' at all.

Some types of spectacles spawned considerable followings in their day and remain cult collectibles for today's antique enthusiasts – many but by no means all of them opticians – who swell the ranks of the Britain-based Ophthalmic Antiques International Collectors' Club and its North American equivalent, the Ocular Heritage Society.

There are no surviving frames from the earliest spectacles, which literary references suggest evolved in the later thirteenth century. Spectacles seem to have been largely the preserve of monks and nuns, for reasons that are threefold: the inhabitants of monastic houses could read, making them more likely to seek corrective vision aids as their sight deteriorated; they had better medical care and were therefore more likely to live beyond the age of forty, when presbyopia, or age-related long-sightedness (the only condition the earliest ophthalmic lenses could correct), kicks in; and they owned the landed estates on which roamed the herds of cattle that were the source of the materials – leather and bone – used to make spectacle frames.

In the later Middle Ages the French spectacle makers adopted St Jerome as their patron saint. This man's impeccable holy and scholarly credentials went some way to rehabilitating the idea of spectacle-wearing, which had suffered owing to the tendency of artists to include spectacles in portraits as a device for criticizing their subjects on grounds of venality, miserliness or excessive zeal for unpopular officialdom.

Centres for high-quality spectacle making developed in many European cities, particularly those that were also known for their links with the book trade, such as Nuremberg in Bavaria, where we know of spectacle makers from 1478. In Germany prices were fixed by statute in 1583, and the sale of cheap spectacles was prohibited. In seventeenth-century London the Worshipful Company of Spectacle Makers made inspection visits that were almost as scary as those of the Spanish Inquisition, and could confiscate any substandard spectacle frames found on sale and smash them ceremonially with a hammer on the ancient London Stone in Cannon Street. Spectacle makers were trained by apprenticeship, and the masterpieces of Nuremberg and Regensburg

A patient information brochure published by the Optical Information Council in the 1950s, showing spectacle wearers engaged in everyday life and at work.

Left, top to bottom: A vertical oval frame echoing eighteenth-century styles, by Metzler (Germany, 1970s); Op-Art spectacles with striped 'canopy' (probably French, *c.* 1950); a very early fashion frame with lace embedded in the plastic (possibly British, 1940s); an anodised metal frame with appliqué trim, by Tura Eyewear (American, mid-twentieth century).

Maskerade (1955), by the British firm Ian Prince, introduced interchangeable trims, an early attempt at 'lifestyle dispensing'.

An aluminium frame of the 1960s, from the Tura company, which was a member of the Fashion Eyewear Group of America established in 1964. Tura's aluminium frames were very attractive but difficult to adjust. The firm's basic rim shapes could be anodised to produce a range of colours, and numerous auxiliary trims were available. In the early 1960s Tura's Barton Levoy travelled the world offering 'Tura School' lectures on fashion dispensing.

Imitation-wood Italian Filos frames, 1960s. Such plastic frames sold remarkably well in the 1960s. They were imported for Britain's Oliver Goldsmith spectacle makers, demonstrating how manufacturing brands often sustained their business through distribution deals with other brands.

Maui Jim started life in the early 1980s as a range of sunglasses, such as this pair, that was sold on the beaches of Hawaii, and developed into a major international brand. The company's later products have often been made in titanium.

makers are particularly noteworthy for their filigree carving, which demonstrates the height of their skills. Some spectacle makers acquired fame and reputation. The renowned diarist Samuel Pepys recorded in October 1667: 'Bought me two new pair of spectacles of Turlington, who, it seems, is famous for them'.

None of these spectacles had sides. There had been earlier attempts to tie spectacles to the head by cords, but sides do not appear to have been invented before the second decade of the eighteenth century, possibly by Edward Scarlett of Soho. Although these spectacles would be difficult to wear today, since their sides were designed to enter into the folds of a wig, we do at least see the beginnings of continuous-use eyewear. Benjamin Martin of London designed an immensely popular style in the 1750s. His innovation was to introduce an inner rim of horn or shell, reducing the aperture of the lens to a small size, ostensibly for optical reasons and to cut out extraneous light but with the principal effect of altering distinctly the outward appearance of the wearer. Martin traded under the sign of his 'Visual Glasses', about which he also wrote, noting that they were 'vulgarly called spectacles'. In effect he had captured the style of an era, and examples of what collectors today call 'Martin's Margins' were still being worn a century after their introduction.

From the late eighteenth century the hitherto slow evolution of eyewear styles was stimulated by a rash of innovations in technological design. In Britain, James Ayscough designed double-hinged sides around 1752, in 1783 Addison Smith took

F4-53 'Move' rimless design (2010), by the French jeweller Fred, which launched its eyewear line in 1988. The branding is clearly marked on the pads but, as befits a work of jewellery, it is almost invisible on the outer sides. On dispensing, the client's prescription lenses would, of course, replace the marked display lenses.

Swatch Eyes 519-062, from 1993, 'for all eyes which have been looking enviously at the world's wrists', made under licence from the Swatch watch brand. The basic frame could be varied with different clip-on components.

Calvin Klein CK603S in imitation tortoiseshell, 1990s. As many other designers have done, Calvin Klein has licensed third parties to use his name on eyewear. Some commentators feel that the practice carries the risk that the brand will be devalued. Licences are frequently shifted from one manufacturer to another, making tracing the history of an eyewear brand all the more complicated.

Eley Kishimoto EK F1, 2004. The true creators of cult eyewear are often unsung. These sunglasses branded Eley Kishimoto (Mark Eley and Wakako Kishimoto) were produced by Linda Farrow, one of the 'brand producers' who supply eyewear under various designers' names.

Alyson Magee S1S070112S, 2007. The 'branches' at the end of the sides are studded with Swarovski stones. Many designers produce work anonymously for established brands. Alyson Magee, based in London and Paris, has designed for Alain Mikli, Anglo American, Lafont and Face-à-Face, and continues to work for one of the luxury fashion houses. She launched her own-name brand in 2007.

out the first recorded patent for spectacles (GB1389) and in 1797 John Richardson patented side visors for auxiliary lenses that could be brought into use when required. Offshoots of this type of eyewear, D-spectacles, emerged around the 1820s and subsequently found popularity among those brave souls who ventured on to the passenger railway carriage – an exciting new form of transport that was open to the wind, the smoke of the funnel and sparks off the track. In France in the 1820s the notion was that spectacles should be as inconspicuous as possible, and 'invisibles', where the thinnest of wire frames was embedded in a grooved edge in each lens, were produced in the area of Les Rousses, in the eastern region of the Jura.

We may contrast 'invisibles' with the highly visible styles of the twentieth century. The first fashion editorial to feature a model wearing sunglasses is thought to have appeared in *Harper's Bazaar* magazine in 1938, and in the late 1940s the German optical industry, seeking to reach a wider market, adopted the slogan 'See better – look better' (*Besser sehen – besser aussehen*). Glasses were now sold as lifestyle accessories. In the United States Foster Grant introduced the retail carousel so that customers could browse the selection more easily, and the Austrian brands led the way for branded window displays, including customized stands and posters supplied free to opticians stocking their products.

Distinct areas of dispensing arose: prescription spectacles (also known as optical frames); sunglasses; sports eyewear, such as Vuarnet (p. 93), Revo,

Arnette and Oakley; and luxury eyewear, such as Gucci, Cartier (p. 35) and Bulgari. Many of today's most prominent high-street brands are surprisingly recent arrivals on the shelves: Chanel, for instance, produced its first sunglasses in 1965 but entered the market properly only in 1999. Far from being a 'distress purchase', shaming their wearers, spectacles now contributed towards retail therapy. Fashion houses, film studios and tobacco companies all got in on the act. Vintage styles offered a different form of comfort, and in 1997 Dunelm even named a range simply Retro. The acquisition in 1995 by the Italian Luxottica Group of LensCrafters, North America's biggest retail optical chain, followed by Sunglass Hut in 2001, meant that it became the first frame manufacturer to enter the retail market directly.

Many of the brands featured in this book now run their own boutiques; others can be bought only from opticians' practices. Eyewear brands have established fan websites, blogs and Facebook pages, and have engaged in viral marketing campaigns. A lucky fan might even displace a celebrity as the marketing face of the brand (see Police, p. 145). Even as the promotional operations grew bigger and slicker, however, in the second decade of the twenty-first century, the first signs were there that, maybe, the future lay in bespoke eyewear and the cult of the individual (see TD Tom Davies, p. 175).

The Austrian firm Silhouette now promotes its online 'Virtual Mirror' as a means of trying on its Aesthetics range (designed in conjunction with British personal stylist Mary Greenwell) from the comfort of your own home, perhaps via a mobile phone.

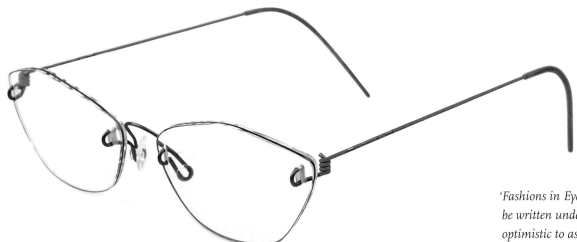

Air Titanium Rim, 1994. The Danish Air Titanium brand, launched in the mid-1980s by optometrist Poul-Jorn Lindberg and architects Dissing & Weitling, was originally sold in just one practice. Some ten years later it accounted for 8 per cent of all frames sold in Denmark, and almost a fifth of the Japanese market. The designers' aim was to avoid distracting from the face. By contrast, the company's Strip Titanium range (1998) was launched in response to demand for a more visible frame.

'Fashions in Eyewear': Can an article be written under this heading, or is it too optimistic to assume that any frame or frames will maintain popularity long enough to stay in fashion whilst this goes to print?

Eric Schaffler, *London Optical News*,
April 1939

C.W. Dixey & Son

The British firm of C.W. Dixey & Son claims to be the oldest independent eyewear company in the world, and the long list of prestigious clients to whom the company has sold spectacles across two centuries includes seven successive British monarchs and members of ten other royal houses. Winston Churchill was a loyal customer for fifty years. Inspired by his rediscovery of lost royal warrants, the current company owner, Simon Palmer, revived the name in the new millenium, issuing its first new eyewear for a generation and reinterpreting the genre for discerning twenty-first-century customers who appreciate both tradition and classic English elegance.

When William Fraser established an optical and mathematical instrument business at 3 New Bond Street, London, in 1777, the exclusive shopping experience differed a little from today's: a cow on the premises provided refreshment to thirsty clients while they perused his diverse selection of products. Fraser was awarded a royal warrant as mathematical instrument maker to George III in 1796, beginning the long relationship with British royalty, although the business went into decline after the Fraser family sold it and the new

owner used the premises for gambling. In 1822 Charles Wastell Dixey (1798–1880) and his uncle George (died 1838) acquired the ailing business and named it G. & C. Dixey (the '& Son' was added about a decade later). The Duke of Wellington would become a client (although he complained on one occasion, when he was sent a spectacle case in the wrong colour), and the partnership was awarded royal warrants from George IV, William IV and the Duchess of Kent. One invoice details six pairs of gold spectacles and a pearl-and-gold case.

After his uncle's death Charles changed the name of the company to C.W. Dixey, the premises serving as his family home, business and workshop. In 1846 he supplied William IV's widow with two pairs of 'square eyed steel spectacles with tinted glasses'. The dowager Queen travelled extensively during this period, but her purchase probably represented a therapeutic tint rather than an early example of royal sunglasses.

In mid-nineteenth-century London aristocrats were offered considerable credit, with a Dixey employee calling at their homes once a year to collect outstanding accounts. It was not unusual for the firm to supply many generations of the same

A drawing of C.W. Dixey's premises from 1777 to 1929, on London's New Bond Street.

Walter Dixey, the last family member to run the company, handed the business over to his staff in 1929.

OPPOSITE
Winston Churchill, British prime minister and MP for Woodford, Essex, addressing a meeting in his constituency in 1952. All his spectacles and sunglasses were made by Dixey.

1

Early twentieth-century Dixey gold specs and leather slip case.

2

A statement made out to the Admiral of the Fleet, the 1st Earl Beatty. He died on 11 March 1936, just two months after this statement was issued.

3

A receipt for a new gold bridge from the early 1890s, a time when spectacles were repaired rather than replaced.

4

A pair of spectacles that belonged to Winston Churchill. Churchill required spectacles for reading, sketching and card playing. In 1944 a 'dot' code was devised to distinguish the different pairs; the one shown here, probably returned for repair, has double dots on the ends. Churchill cancelled his spectacle insurance with Dixey in September 1939, at the start of the Second World War, but within five days of the war ending ordered a new pair for painting.

5

A medal issued by Dixey in 1937 to mark the coronation of George VI. This side depicts an eighteenth-century woman using a lorgnette, seated at a table in conversation with a standing gentleman – possibly her dispensing stylist?

6

A Dixey record card of 1939 for the Empress of Abyssinia.

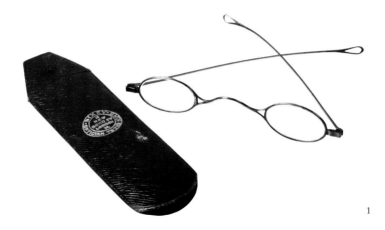

1

2

3

4

5

6

family with eyewear of the finest materials, including silver, gold, ivory and tortoise-shell. After Charles Dixey's death in 1880 the business was carried on by his son, Adolphus, and grandson, Walter. On one occasion Walter, who was the third generation of the Dixey family to serve as optician to Queen Victoria, had to tell Her Majesty that her nose was totally unsuitable for the pince-nez she had demanded. He reportedly returned home 'a little shaken'.

In 1929 the period of family ownership ended. Walter Dixey transferred the ownership of the business to his loyal staff and the firm relocated to 19 Old Bond Street. The firm went to extraordinary lengths to delight clients. Documents record, for example, that a luxury gold-and-platinum eyewear collection was created, variously engraved, enamelled and set with diamonds, and that a brown snakeskin spectacle case was created for the Empress of Abyssinia.

The premises and company archive were destroyed in the London Blitz, forcing Dixey to leave Bond Street after 163 years. It relocated a short distance away, to 20 Welbeck Street in London's medical district. In the 1950s, during the post-war period of austerity, the company started an innovative service known as the 'Regency Room', whereby ladies could commission sophisticated bespoke spectacles under the guidance of an ex-catwalk fashion model. The Pathé film *Spectacles*, shown in British cinemas in 1953, featured such Regency Room frames as designer Betty Spurling's midnight-blue 'flame'-pattern frame with marcasite crescent moons and stars, the Black Magic leaf-pattern frame (described

1

by the film's narrator as 'devilishly tempting'), and a frame named in tribute to its model, Jean Dawnay, who would later marry a Russian prince. During the 1960s C.W. Dixey & Son attracted a new breed of customer, among which were many writers, actors, artists, adventurers and entertainers. Celebrated clients included Ian Fleming, the author of the James Bond novels.

In 1977 Dixey was at the height of its powers, celebrating its two-hundredth anniversary, being granted a coat of arms and commissioning a book on its history. Within a few years, however, the firm faced the greatest challenge in its history, when internal dishonesty nearly destroyed it. Although it survived as an independent family business, it was forced to scale back its operations significantly. Dixey's last retail premises, in south-east London, closed in 2009, but this provided the impetus for the new owners to return to the designer eyewear scene, offering British designs manufactured by family businesses in both England and mainland Europe.

2

3

4

1
A note from actor Peter Sellers in the Dixey visitor book, 1979.

2
A Dixey postage box from the 1940s.

3
Folding tortoiseshell frame, mid-twentieth century.

4
Prototypes of the new Dixey range for 2010.

American Optical

American Optical (AO) dominated the United States lens market in the first half of the twentieth century, and for this reason its innovations in frame designs have sometimes been ignored. The company name dates from 1869 but the firm originated in 1833, when William Beecher of Southbridge, Massachusetts, first offered optical goods in his jewellery shop. Beecher subsequently introduced steel-frame manufacture to the United States, thereby reducing the New World's reliance on European imports. From the 1870s until 1949 the company was dominated by the Wells family. Major innovations in this period were the company's publication of an illustrated catalogue in 1894, and, from before the First World War, the informative *Amoptico* magazine (later renamed *Wellsworth*). Its pages demonstrate that AO was into 'lifestyle dispensing' years ahead of its time.

AO can be deemed to have begun its role in designer eyewear in 1952, when it issued a collection of ninety frames by Italian fashion designer Elsa Schiaparelli (the first designer eyewear collection to be launched in the United States), including a diamond-studded platinum frame termed 'the Crown Jewels'. Earlier flamboyant frames of Schiaparelli design with blue feathered 'eyelashes' had been pictured in *Life* magazine back in 1951. She liked to ask her artist friends to design strange objects for her – 'amusements', as she called them – including white spectacle frames shaped like daisies. In addition to this pioneering attempt to work with an established fashion name, AO set up its own frame studio in an expanded cupboard, employing two graduates of the Rhode Island School of Design.

In 1957 the company underwent a significant strategic change, with new sales-orientated blood being brought in from outside the optical industry. The influential Victor Kniss from the Westinghouse Electric Corporation took over, bringing many of his branch managers with him.

In 1958 AO, under Frank Nadeau, developed for the US Air Force the Flight Goggle 58 (FG-58), now known as the Original Pilot Sunglass, or OPS. Historical details are sketchy because Nadeau regarded the design as his personal

American Optical's *Wellworth* magazine from 1916, offering eyewear for specific sporting and leisure purposes. It features one of the earliest identified references to 'sun glasses'.

American Optical's Numont frame, introduced in 1940 and manufactured in other countries as well as in the United States, on an original retail card. The Numont mount had a slightly visible upper rim that was positioned behind the lens.

OPPOSITE:
Sunvogue Model 8172, in a catalogue image from 1969.

23

project and therefore little is in the public domain, but the FG-58 also became the frame of choice for the US Army (the 'Top Guns' of the US Navy preferred their Ray-Bans; see p. 67), and astronaut Neil Armstrong took a pair with him on the Apollo 11 mission, which landed the first humans on the moon in 1969. The OPS is still manufactured near the original AO complex in Southbridge, Massachusetts, by AO Eyewear. European production of the aviator, pilot and navigator frames took place in France until 1991, when it moved to Britain's Algha Works (see p. 55). The OPS was offered to the British market for the first time only in 1992, targeted at the under-thirties customer. That venture was discontinued a few years later, but at one point 4000 'American' sunglasses a month were being produced in London.

American Optical was also known at home for its Cool-Ray sunglasses in the late 1940s and its Sunvogue collection of the 1960s, which incorporated either Calobar, Cosmetan or True Color branded lenses. AO described Sunvogues as the '"in"

sunglasses that you'll find the go-crowd wearing', and gave the models names rather than numbers. The women's range included Promenade and Pebble Beach, evoking a destination for the would-be wearer, and (for a black-and-white frame reminiscent of the Op-Art frames so popular in Europe at the time) Torrid; they were advertised as being 'for the woman who dares to be different ... and those who are thinking about it'. The men's range was promoted as combining 'a masculine fashion flair with manly practical ruggedness'.

In the 1970s, consciously distinguishing its product from cheap sunglasses, the company contrasted its well-engineered, reinforced frames with those 'slide-down-your-nose-push-them-up-again' frames. Sunvogues were offered in colours with such 'natural'-sounding names as coral, pecan, grape, mint and cranberry ... all items you'd expect to flourish under the nurturing sun.

1
An American Optical frame catalogue, 1962.

2
A catalogue for AO's Sunvogue collection, 1966.

3
Two Sunvogue sunglasses: Bayside for men and Sultry for women, 1974.

4
Tiffany women's frame, post-1972.

5
Andorra women's frame, post-1959.

Anglo American

Thoroughly British and yet transatlantic in both origin and outlook, Anglo American existed by 1881; no one is quite sure when it came into being, but it was around that time that Englishman Stanley Druiff set off for the United States to buy fountain pens, watches and spectacles to sell back in Britain. Only the last line succeeded. In about 1947 the company was bought from Druiff's descendants by optician Arthur Jenkin. With the establishment of the National Health Service in 1948, demand for frames increased dramatically, so from then on Anglo American concentrated on frames, although primarily as a prescription house. Imports from the United States, which had ceased during the Second World War, resumed in 1955, with 'styled' frames from the likes of Tura, Whitney and Gaspari.

Arthur Jenkin's son, Lawrence (born 1943), who wanted to make frames, left Britain in 1967 to learn the trade in New York, where he worked first as a dispenser for the high-class optical practice of Lugene,

1

2

3

4

1
Early Anglo American advertising emphasized elegance of appearance and range of materials.

2
The flat-topped OC101 (1991) sold well to musicians. Its tailored look was the result of Anglo American's barrelling technique, which did not smooth off the sharp edges. AA also offered a version that was surmounted by a rolling pin.

3
Lawrence Jenkin, the creative force behind the AA brand, always acknowledged the contribution of his brothers, Malcolm and Tony, and aimed to promote the company, not the individuals within it. Only now, in his sixth decade of spectacle making, is he operating a business under his own name.

4
OC102, 1990s. For AA the back of the frame was as important as the front, and the sides were always considered to be part of the design.

OPPOSITE
The Fontana frame in black, from a catalogue of 1991.

Butterfly, part of the Alternative collection, 1970s.

Detroit, part of the New Direction range, late 1980s.

Joker with bells, from the Card series, 1980s.

Lips, 1982.

in the heart of the business district, then for Vision Unlimited, which claimed to be the first optical boutique, on Third Avenue. Both businesses attracted film-star clients, and Jenkin dispensed to both Paul Newman (who was always losing his sunglasses) and an ageing Greta Garbo. Popular frames included those by Oliver Goldsmith (p. 49) and the NHS C223 children's frame, which was in fact a favourite among American adults. Jenkin also did some freelance design for Whitney Optical, and he won prizes in a frame-design competition run by the Fashion Eyewear Group of America (now defunct). Vision Unlimited offered him $24,000 to establish his own factory, which he set up at his father's premises in London in 1970.

Thus, backed by American money, Anglo American manufactured frames in volume for the first time. The firm made basic shapes, but in a larger size than was common at the time, and, rather than using the extrusion process, worked Italian Mazzucchelli acetate and French Rhône-Poulenc materials by the block method. Whereas at that point – the early 1970s – Oliver Goldsmith sold only to the UK, Anglo American struggled to sell at home (for a while its only client was Cutler and Gross; p. 113) but did very well in the United States and also sold well to Germany and Austria (where it forged links with Viennaline; p. 87), Belgium (where among its clients were the founders of theo; p. 151), The Netherlands and France. The *Ophthalmic Optician* reported in April 1978 (by which time Arthur Jenkin had taken a back seat in the running of the company) that 'until recently' the company had been

1
Sydney Olympics 2000 –
available long ahead of the
event, *c.* 1994.

2
Odeon Panto, *c.* 1992.

3
Fontana, late 1980s.

4
Snake, date unknown.

5
Coquille, pre-1991.

6
Frog, 1991.

The 132 model, in grey, rose, purple and indigo, featured on the cover of a Harrods brochure in 1985. It was yours for £43. Lawrence Jenkin's mother, Evelyn (Eve), who had a background in pottery design, did the dyeing for the multicolour range.

Swans, date unknown.

Model 237 with keyform bridge, early 1990s.

primarily an exporter but was now experiencing home growth.

By the 1980s Lawrence Jenkin and his brother Malcolm, a toolmaker, were running Anglo American, which had offices in London, New York and Tokyo. Another brother, Tony, came in to handle sales; in the United States the firm's frames were distributed by Sir Winston Eyewear of California, and were sold at Bloomingdale's and all the other American department stores. During this period the company was making most frames in two sizes, the larger size for sun glazing. In 1986 Anglo American opened its first branch in the United States, on New York's Park Avenue, under the name Anglo American Eyewear in order to reflect its status as a fashion eyewear manufacturer, and this name was thereafter also used in Britain.

Lawrence Jenkin had always been keen on vintage eyewear. In about 1983, as European agent for Shuron, he imported and launched in Europe the American company's Ronsir model, a top fashion combination frame of the 1950s with a heavy black browbar. Then in 1986 Jenkin launched his New Direction range under the straightforward slogan 'Back to the 50s'. Unlike the styles that inspired them, these frames were not all handmade but involved a lot of handwork; the idea was to convey a vintage 'resonance' (for example, the range made use of 1930s pinned joints sourced from Switzerland) while providing a more fashionable shape and colour.

By the early 1990s Anglo American employed about sixty people, and, although the firm was trying to get away from the hand-tinted, oversized frames that had been so popular in the 1980s, it was the main surviving acetate-frame manufacturer in Britain. Corporate publicity claimed that Anglo American was 'one of the last few British frame manufacturers to continue to export and expand worldwide', and boasted that, with each frame being handled at least seventy-five times in forty-three operations, and being checked a minimum of fifteen times, 'it may not be the cheapest way to make a frame but for Anglo American Eyewear it is the only way'.

Anglo American is known to collectors today for its Alternative collection, which began in the early 1970s with the butterfly; this frame was produced in order to gain coverage in magazines, but sold in surprising numbers. The collection's main purpose was to bring people to the company stand at trade shows. Most models were too difficult to make entirely by hand, so the company brought in an accomplished toolmaker from the toy firm Lesney. In 1991–92 the collection expanded to include

Dame Edna Everage

'Housewife and gigastar', played by Australian comedian/actor Barry Humphries (born 1934)

Sketch for a dress designed for Dame Edna by costume designer Stephen Adnitt and Barry Humphries, featuring a profile of the character in flamboyant eyewear. In the finished dress, the spectacles were made of plastazote foam and covered in fabric.

Almost any extravagant frame can be described these days as a 'Dame Edna' type, in reference to the comic character created by the Australian actor Barry Humphries. 'Mrs' Edna Everage was far from flamboyant when she first appeared on stage in 1955: the earliest surviving photograph of her, from 1958, shows that Humphries portrayed her as a suburban housewife – without spectacles.

Eyewear appeared at Humphries's first solo show in 1962, in which Edna wore butterfly spectacles with a pinch of diamanté for a sharper look, and they became a staple part of her outfit in the mid-1960s. In those days she sometimes also wore pink glasses, or a Perspex supra with upswept leaf trim. The spectacles were bought from opticians, picked up in thrift shops, or provided by Humphries's friend Stephanie Deste, a beautician and broadcaster who imported French frames for her chain of salons in Melbourne.

Humphries's Australian characters were first presented to British audiences in 1963,

and achieved success later that decade in the BBC's *The Late Show*, by which time Edna's eyewear was established. Edna was glammed up in the early 1970s, becoming a parody of high fashion with outfits that included ever more extravagant spectacles, many of them bought in Parisian flea markets in the 1960s and 1970s; sadly, most were lost in the early 1980s by a negligent manager.

Dame Edna has always claimed that her costumes, including her 'face furniture', were designed by her son Kenny. In fact, from 1985 costume designer Stephen Adnitt was responsible for her outfits on her television series. Adnitt designed a pair of spectacles to go with each dress, working from two shapes: 'flames' (of which Humphries already made use) and his own 'curls', which he has said he wishes he had patented, because the motif was later used by the MAC cosmetics firm as the packaging symbol for a range of products. Humphries had earlier discovered Anglo American spectacles, and he introduced Adnitt to Lawrence Jenkin.

For a skit about the Australian television series *Prisoner Cell Block H* the firm made an upside-down snooker frame with prison bars, and, for a picture for the front cover of *Radio Times*, it made a frame in the shape of the letters R and T. None of Dame Edna's spectacles was glazed, since for a comedian it is important that the eyes be fully visible, especially when playing a comic character involving so much facial expression. Once Humphries had established the optimum internal rim aperture, the size never changed.

AA used to inscribe the sides of Dame Edna's spectacles (which were handmade for her) with the humorous line 'A hand job by Anglo American' or 'By appointment to Dame Edna'. More recently, former Anglo American frame maker David Cox has been engaged with Adnitt to work on Humphries's Tony Award-winning Broadway stage shows.

The 'Look' frame (c. 1986) used Rocel colours from the Courtaulds company.

such classic styles as the frog and the shark, wacky designs that are now themselves considered to be vintage. Some of Lawrence Jenkin's best work was yet to come: he won the Spectacle Makers Company 'Frame of the Year' award in 1993 for his Camarillo sunglasses, and again in 1994 for the Airlite 403, a frame produced in very thin acetate.

But in 1995 Anglo American had to be saved financially by New York optometrist Dr Ken Roth, and the company's New York office was closed. Mindful of the need to retain the British custom, Anglo American exhibited at Optrafair for the first time in ten years. The following year Lawrence Jenkin left the company, and he now continues to work on a number of personal projects. In 2000 Tony Jenkin's company, Pro-ID, took over the firm to lead it into its third century.

Lima, part of the New Direction range, pre-1991.

Sirmont, part of the Lightweight range, pre-1991.

Bat, c. 1991.

Curvebar, *c.* 1994.

Award-winning model 404, *c.* 1993.

Camarillo (far left), from 1993 but reminiscent of the heavy, slightly upswept frames of the 1960s. The frame, designed by Lawrence Jenkin, assisted by Alyson Magee, won Britain's Spectacle Maker's Company 'Frame of the Year' award. Its unisex design suited moulding, but in fact it was carved from 22-mm (7/8-7in.) acetate. Jenkin was quoted as saying, 'It shows that we have the ability to make anything.'

Pterodactyl (*c.* 1991) more closely resembles a pteranodon.

Cartier

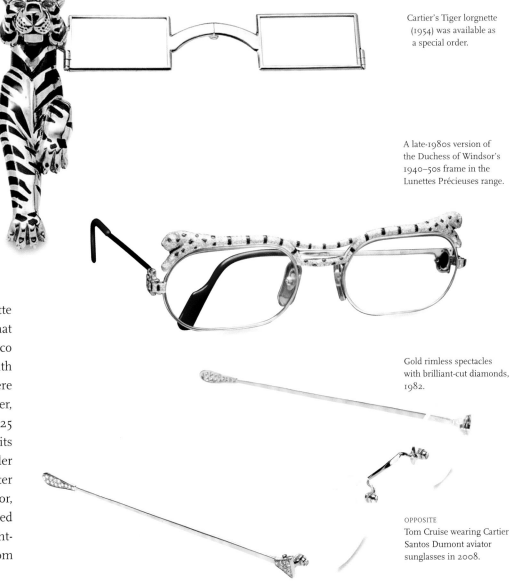

When in 1887 the French jewellery firm Cartier made a lorgnette for the Princess of Essling, there was nothing inevitable about its subsequent foray into optics. But thanks to an increasing number of one-off commissions (primarily for magnifying glasses), by the eve of the First World War Cartier maintained a specialist optical department on Paris's prestigious rue de la Paix, and its clients included high society's most feted individuals. In the late 1920s the 2nd Duke of Westminster ordered a lorgnette in platinum with diamonds and pearls that he presented to the fashion designer Coco Chanel, but it didn't get him very far with her; she is supposed to have said that there had been several duchesses of Westminster, but there was only one Chanel. In 1925 Cartier supplied what are believed to be its first spectacles to Jeanne Lanvin, founder of the Lanvin fashion house. Cartier later made for Wallis, the Duchess of Windsor, spectacles that featured two panthers joined tail-to-tail on the browbar, with wrought-platinum bodies featuring spots made from

Cartier's Tiger lorgnette (1954) was available as a special order.

A late-1980s version of the Duchess of Windsor's 1940–50s frame in the Lunettes Précieuses range.

Gold rimless spectacles with brilliant-cut diamonds, 1982.

OPPOSITE
Tom Cruise wearing Cartier Santos Dumont aviator sunglasses in 2008.

Cartier promotional material: Right, from the launch of Must de Cartier Eyewear at Port El Kantaoui, Tunisia, 1983. The phrase *les must de Cartier*, indicating a must-have product, was first used in the 1970s for non-jewellery products, into which Cartier was diversifying. Far right, an advertisement of 1987 for the Santos frame, which was part of a range of luxury accessories that included lighters, pens and the distinctive men's square wristwatch. The first of these watches was designed for Louis Cartier's friend Alberto Santos-Dumont in 1904.

This Santos model was purchased in Spain as a pair of sunglasses, but the owner liked it so much that he had it converted to prescription use, and it now sports what is clearly a set of bifocals.

These sunglasses, dated 2005, from the C Décor collection (launched in 2000) shows that a rimless frame can still feature solid-gold components. The sides are made of 'zebra-pattern' bubinga (*Guibourtia demeusei*), an African wood also used by Lexus for its luxury car interiors.

Masculine Sunwear (2006), with prominent metal screw motif.

onyx and emeralds for eyes, and the duchess's Cartier tiger-handle lorgnette was featured in *Vogue* in 1954.

In 1983 Cartier launched its modern Cartier Eyewear range, manufactured under licence by the French firm Essilor. This included the Must and Vendome frames, available in 18-carat gold and set with diamonds, rubies, emeralds and sapphires. Unlike most of the first wave of modern luxury brands, Cartier's licence agreement retained control of the design and production, which took place at the company's workshops in Joinville-le-Pont, south-east of Paris. In 1997 Cartier established its own luxury eyewear division; a spokeswoman revealed much when she offered the opinion that Cartier frames were so opulent that many customers never actually wore them. Security has been an understandable concern: all Cartier frames have a serial number so that they can be traced if recovered by the police, and, as a precaution against fakes, in some frames, such as the Romance frame of 1987, the lenses revealed the Cartier 'C' when breathed on.

Cartier's original 1983 range comprised fifteen frames, and opticians who wanted to stock Cartier had to take the whole range. The complex tooling involved in Cartier spectacles has meant that new models have seldom been added. In February 1987 the UK sales manager was quoted in *The Optician* as saying 'We don't follow fashion, so never become dated.' Design innovations have included the half-eye frame introduced in 1987 and an acetate range launched in 1996, as well as a jewellery collection inspired by the sales of the Duchess of

Windsor's estate in 1987. The six models included the Panthère, the Impériale (an elongated oval shape with a diamond-and-ruby browbar) and an aviator style, the Princesse, featuring three rows of 119 diamonds in its triple browbar. Opticians could order these models (on an eight-week turnaround) but not keep them in stock; rather, potential purchasers could browse a 'customer-friendly dispensing aid' – in other words, a catalogue. Reputedly the most expensive sunglasses in the world, the Must Panthère retailed for about £60,000 in 1995; it was offered alongside a lesser jewellery collection, some frames costing less than £10,000, and the rimless, extra-lightweight New Generation Eyewear, which came in 'feminine oval', 'sassy round' and 'sensible square' shapes suitable for prescription use. There was also a solid-gold range, and the company offered training to opticians so they would not panic if a customer expressed an interest in buying a model; in August 1994 it was reported that five had been sold in Britain so far that year.

Half-eye in 22-carat gold (far left) with a Bordeaux lacquer finish, 1987. This model was aimed at the young to middle-aged businessman, which at the time was an unusual target market for this type of frame.

The introduction of acetate in the Composites range widened the choice of Cartier frames after 1996. This model from 1999 is in brown jasper.

The three pin heads add a visible touch of functional interest to an otherwise plain front in black, with ruthenium finish, from the Collection Première (2009).

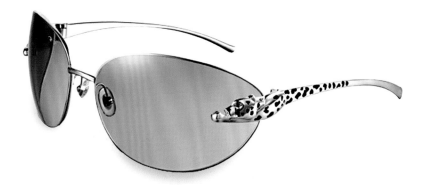

A limited-edition Panthère with smooth platinum finish, from 2009. This model was restricted to 2000 pieces.

Kirk Brothers | Kirk Originals

The name Kirk Originals requires explanation. In truth, there have been two historic Kirk brands: a creative interwar partnership between two inspired British brothers, and a descendant's later revival based on genuine vintage frames. Seldom has a company been so proud of its history, yet so clearly disinclined to be governed by that heritage.

In 1919 Sidney and Percy Kirk, two ex-dairy farmers, established themselves in London, where they manufactured various items, including buttons that they supplied to Woolworths. Never averse to taking work home with them, they converted a sewing machine into a lens cutter. Encouraged by Max Wiseman of optical instrument business M. Wiseman & Co., who later founded the Algha Works (see p. 55), the Kirk brothers concentrated on optics and in 1920 established a frames-manufacturing business on Gray's Inn Road, eventually employing one hundred people. Between 1925 and 1935 they took out ten patents for improvements in pads, mountings and pince-nez.

Sidney Kirk was apparently the more 'hands-on' brother, while Percy handled the marketing. Kirk Brothers was the first British optical company to have a publicity department and, in 1929, the first to employ motorcycle couriers. The Kirbro brand offered various products prefixed 'Kir', such as the Kirbend side-measuring rule. After the Second World War the brothers split; Percy continued as a wholesaler in his own name (retaining the brothers' Motex safety-goggle business, which he moved to Devon, where it later merged with the Salvoc firm), and Sidney started the Kirk Optical Co. in Hatton Garden, London's 'jewellery street'.

Sidney Kirk had five sons and one daughter, Dena, who in her day became the country's sole optical saleswoman. One son, Neville, practised as an optician, first in partnership with his brothers, then on his own in the small Buckinghamshire town of Chalfont St Giles. In 1992 Neville and his son Jason discovered some old interwar Kirk frames in the practice, and shortly afterwards Jason had the good fortune (as he later saw it) to be made redundant from his marketing role at L'Oréal. Having visited London opticians to ensure that nothing similar was on offer, Jason entered the family optical tradition, re-glazing the old-fashioned styles with modern sunglass

The Kirk brothers, Percy (far left) and Sidney, with their wives, in a photograph dating from between the world wars.

OPPOSITE
Chip, from Kirk Originals' Kinetic collection, 2010.

Early Kirk Brothers frames were of calcite, a milk-based plastic. Allegedly an early Kirk model, this interwar frame from the British Optical Association Museum bears no distinguishing marks (which is not unusual for the period) but does not match the shapes illustrated in the firm's print advertisements. The authenticity of the attribution must therefore be deemed unproven.

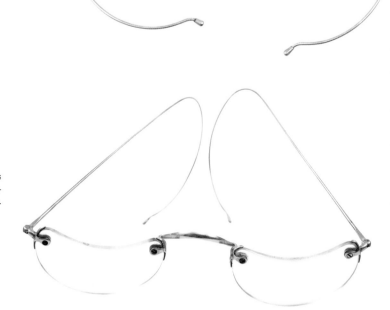

Kirk's Facifit one-piece metal pad bridge, patented in 1927, was fitted to a variety of frame shapes. The bridge later featured rocking pads.

Kirbro three-piece rimless half-eye with crescent-shaped lenses, 1930s.

lenses and selling them through quirky boutiques, such as those of designers Helen Storey and Nick Coleman. Jason has described this mixing of old and new ingredients as the optical equivalent of alchemy. He eventually ran out of original frames, of course, but bought old stocks of acetate sheet so that new frames could be made from original materials: 1960s styling from 1960s plastic.

In 1993 Jason married Karen, a graphic designer, who became his partner in the business, and the couple started designing their own frames. The Kirk Originals range of sunglasses debuted at the French SILMO trade show in 1994 and soon won a Japanese award. Initially, the Kirks ran the business from their living room (pieces of Lego occasionally found their way into customers' deliveries, surreptitiously placed there by the Kirks' young son), but in 1996 the company opened its own shop and offices in the popular London shopping district of Covent Garden. It also set up Kirk Originals Manufacture (KOM), a factory for handmaking spectacles frames, in the Essex coastal town of Clacton-on-Sea. In the late 1990s KOM worked with lads'

From the Sculpture range launched in 2000.

The Vector range (2010) introduced the concept of movement in a static object. The spectacles were hand-painted (using a 'secret' ingredient) so that the colour appeared to meander along the frame if it were turned towards light.

1

Hilary Kirk was one of the fictitious historic Kirk family members created to accompany the Heroes range launched in 2004.

2

Java, from Kirk Originals' Kinetic collection (2010), in which frame names were inspired by the world of technology. Other names included Byte and Cookie. The firm claimed this was the first-ever 'animated' eyewear range, featuring panel designs that brought depth to the sides, such as a living 'spectrum' of colour, a shooting 'flash' arrow and a strip of blazing flames.

3

British-designed, but now made in France, the Turbo Collection of 2009 combined aluminium, wood and acetate, and featured a racing stripe on the side. This model is in 'tornado brown'.

4

Jason Kirk, grandson of one of the two brothers who founded the Kirk Brothers firm, now runs Kirk Originals with his wife, Karen. He has said that he stopped being surprised at the 'mature' age of some of his clients once he turned forty himself.

HILARY KIRK

Hilary made her fortune in the early 16th century through her invention of the novelty egg cup. A fierce advocate of women's rights, on 31st December 1569 she famously called Henry VIII a 'spineless chauvinist pig'. She died later that year.

PAGE 25 Hilary Kirk

1

2

3

4

mag *Loaded* to produce a Loaded Eyewear range, which included limited-edition sunglasses featuring original 1950s aluminium sides from Switzerland.

In 1999 the Kirk Originals shop suffered a major fire and, although the business survived, years of very difficult trading ensued, latterly as a franchise. Only in 2010 did the firm revive the concept of a directly run boutique in London's West End. The premises comprised a single display wall of frames, and no other furniture that might distract the customer. The business administration has moved to Brighton, while manufacturing is now in the Jura region of France because it is easier to source the necessary component parts there.

Kirk Originals' operating philosophy, 'Try to start with something that's impossible', has influenced the company's preference for unusual materials. For example, the Sculpture collection, launched in 2000, had acetate fronts but acrylic sides that bent round the front; it took three years to develop this acrylic material, and the firm then had to educate opticians in how to explain it to their clients. The company even made a film, *The Look of Love* (posted on YouTube), showing how to adjust the acrylic sides. Kirk Originals now makes many of the materials used in the frames, such as the glitter acetate used for the Shine collection, the concept for which was born when Jason Kirk spilled fruit juice on a frame and noted the textural effect wrought by the acetic acid in the juice.

Vintage-inspired eyewear from Kirk Originals has proved popular with such celebrities as Elton John and Julia Roberts, but the company has always steered clear

Karen (top), Diablo (centre) and Miriam, all from 1995. The Karen cat's-eye frame elicited a massive response after the brand was featured on the BBC's *The Clothes Show* later that year.

of celebrity endorsements, emphasizing that if these people wear Kirk Originals frames it is because they want to, not because they have been paid to do so. In recent years the brand's cult following has been measurable online: in the Kirk Heroes range (launched in 2004), characterized by asymmetric designs that are handmade and hand-painted, each model was based on a fictitious historic Kirk family member as illustrated by Sharie Edwards, and each 'character' had its own Facebook account so that fans could keep up with its activities. Each frame was supplied to the customer with a pack of cards introducing the whole 'family', including Olaf 'the Shadow' Kirk, stunt double for Noël Coward, 'left-handed contortionist' Melissa Kirk and bounty hunter Curly Kirk and her three-legged horse. The heroes soon had more fans than there were actual customers, and by popular demand a 'new generation' of characters, drawn by illustrator and writer Max Scratchmann, was launched in 2009.

Persol

The Italian eyewear industry, the majority of which is based in the Dolomites mountain range in the north-east of the country, owes one of its most enduring brands to the city of Turin in the north-west. Italy's 'capital of the Alps' was also the home of the country's motor manufacturing (Fiat was founded there in 1899 and Lancia in 1906), providing the right background of rapid industrialization, coupled with a rugged environment, to spawn a market for protective eyewear.

Motorists and mountain aviators needed special lenses, and in 1917 Giuseppe Ratti, owner of the not very Italian-sounding Berry optician and photographic shop on Turin's Via Roma, began experimenting with smoked tints. The lenses, supported by rubber rims and elastic headbands, were known as Protectors. An early advocate was the writer, daredevil adventurer and First World War fighter pilot Gabriele D'Annunzio, who as the result of a flying accident was blind in one eye. He wore a bespoke Protector when he led a flight of planes to drop propaganda leaflets over the Austrian capital in August 1918 – the so-called 'Flight over Vienna' (*il volo su Vienna*).

These protective spectacles with yellow lenses and vented side visors date from before Persol was founded. Company founder Giuseppe Ratti began experimenting with smoked tints in 1917, but the Persol brand name was not used before 1938.

A first-edition Persol 009 from the 1950s, with patented Meflecto flexible sides. This 'four-lens' model was supplied to early NASA space missions, although the American market was not really conquered before 1962.

A prototype of the folding Persol 714 (*c.* 1940s), in black plastic. The crystal lenses were hand-engraved, and the frames were hand-finished with gold lettering. White lettering is a mark of a later date.

OPPOSITE
Steve McQueen in *The Thomas Crown Affair* (1968), wearing a Persol 714.

This 1950s aviator frame with keyhole bridge featured interchangeable 'Persolmatic' lenses.

Persol chamfered style 6423 (date unknown), with label bearing the stork symbol of company founder Giuseppe Ratti.

The Persol 649, introduced in 1957, with folding bridge. The lenses' strength was checked by dropping a 16-gram (¹/₂-oz) steel weight on to them from a fixed height.

Retro-style Persol 653 (date unknown), featuring the Persol 'Supreme Arrow' straddling the joints.

In the 1920s Ratti developed yellow-brown lenses from a pure silica crystal that proved ideal for absorbing solar rays. These sunglasses came to bear a name that summed up their function as *per il sole* (for the sun), and were promoted by cartoonist Eugenio Colmo's *cinesino* ('little Chinaman'), bedecked with dark-tinted round-eye spectacles. (Although it was an enduring advertising image, lasting several decades, the *cinesino*'s eyewear bore little relation to the actual design of the product.) Early Persol frames were produced in small volume but in a choice of four sizes, and to a degree might almost be considered to be a made-to-measure product. To maximize comfort, particular attention was paid to the edging beneath the bridge.

In 1938 Ratti patented the first flexible side, the Meflecto, and in optical shop windows Persol frames were often displayed stretched out to demonstrate this feature. The idea was that, by virtue of little cylinders of metal or nylon that were inserted vertically through the temple-piece and then intersected with a flexible steel core running along the interior of each side (which was more akin to a plastic watch strap than a rigid side), the sides would hug the wearer's head, resulting in a comfortable fit. It was a logical move to extend this principle to the nasal area, and the Persol 649, introduced in 1957, is the classic frame featuring this notched three-section bridge. The final distinctive feature of Meflectos (and most Persols) from then on, patented in several countries, was the arrow straddling the joints; this was an early instance of an easily recognized decorative element, but it also had a functional purpose in holding the frame together. In its original form it was supposed to represent a warrior's sword, and may therefore be regarded as the cutting edge of Italian eyewear.

The cinema has captured some of Persol's most memorable moments. The 649, originally produced for Turin's tram drivers, was worn by Marcello Mastroianni in the role of Ferdinando Cefalù, prospective wife killer, in the film *Divorzio all' italiana* (*Divorce, Italian Style*, 1961). The sophisticated cigar in a holder, the neat moustache and the smart sunglasses all contributed to making his character appear almost reasonable, and maybe even justified, in his crime of passion. The American actor Steve McQueen typifies the period of Persol's heyday: he wore both the 649 and the folding model 714 in *The Thomas Crown Affair* (1968). In 2006, at an auction staged by Bonhams in Los Angeles, a buyer paid $70,200 (about £36,700) for a pair of sunglasses in mottled imitation shell with keyhole bridge and blue tinted lenses that was believed to have been worn in that film.

The line for *The Thomas Crown Affair* began 'He was young, handsome, a millionaire – and he'd just pulled off the perfect crime', and there does seem to be something about the Persol brand that speaks of the glamour of criminality. The Mini Coopers in the heist movie *The Italian Job* (1969) speed under an illuminated advertisement for Persol; this is appropriate, as the film's plot revolves around a bullion raid in the brand's home city of Turin, with the raid planned to exploit the city's notorious traffic congestion.

In the early 1980s Persol worked with automotive designer Sergio Pininfarina to produce sunglasses (in 'car-type colours') that would appeal to men, but later it branched out into female frames, such as the 830, with shallower, more curvaceous oval rims, and the butterfly-shaped Carol 853, designed for the American model Carol Alt in 1993.

Persol was acquired by the Italian Luxottica Group in 1995, but the brand is still made at its factory in Lauriano, Turin. Many of the production processes continue to require such handcrafting that the company claims that making 'a pair of Persols' takes twice as long as making a pair of ordinary spectacles. More recent models have also appeared in films, such as *Casino Royale* (2006) – James Bond is a good guy, which is perhaps why he later swapped his Persols for a pair by Tom Ford – and *Mamma Mia* (2008), in which Pierce Brosnan wears the 2720-S and commits a crime against singing.

Not only is the Persol brand sometimes not marked on the frame, it also didn't always feature in the advertising, as seen in this 1964 promotion for the Meflecto 803. Note the suggestion that the spectacles be bought as an 'extra pair', at a time when it was a challenge to convince some people to buy even one pair of glasses.

Women's optical frames from 1979.

Persol 848, date unknown.

Persol 40301, date unknown.

Oliver Goldsmith

In 1926 P. (Philip) Oliver Goldsmith (1889–1947), a salesman for the large optical firm Raphaels Ltd, began hand-making spectacles at premises in Poland Street, London, and established his own company to sell them, at 4 guineas a pair. (His former employer recommended the name Oliver, as being more memorable than Philip.) Designs of the era, made in shell, included the Portsmouth, Bull Dog and Adelaide (all from 1928), Elfin, Poland (named after the company's address) and Padishell. Experimenting with the horn-like Erinoid plastic, Goldsmith developed the first flesh-coloured frame, which he called Dawn because it was intended to usher in a new era. The frame's selling point was its supposed unobtrusiveness. By contrast, Goldsmith's Chelsea Art spectacle utilized the same material in a range of colours, notably green.

In 1936 Goldsmith's son, Charles Myer Goldsmith (1914–1991), joined the company, and it was he who recognized the fashion potential of eyewear, becoming a pioneer of the 1950s trend for ornamental frames that coordinated with clothing and featured jewels and metal inserts. After his father's death in 1947 he adopted the name

Oliver for himself, and this second Oliver Goldsmith sold sunglasses to high-class shops, including London's Harrods, Harvey Nichols, Selfridges and Fortnum & Mason. In a move frowned on by most in the optical profession, he also began advertising in such British magazines as *Tatler* and *Harper's Bazaar*, although the brand's first appearance in *Vogue*, in 1954, was unsolicited: an editorial picture appeared there, captioned as 'a face-flattering frame'. In 1956 Goldsmith collaborated with an Italian manufacturer to produce the Goldside, a plain gold side that contrasted wonderfully with a coloured front, to which it was attached by a decorative joint.

The third Goldsmith generation, Andrew Oliver Goldsmith (born 1942), joined the

The second Oliver Goldsmith flanked by his sons Andrew (left) and Raymond, all wearing their signature white suits, at the Grosvenor House trade show, 1967.

Dawn was a pioneering Goldsmith frame of the 1930s and 1940s. This is the reissued version from the 1970s. Note the unreinforced sides.

OPPOSITE
Abstract frame and musical notes frame, both from 1985, made for appearances on American television interviews but never sold.

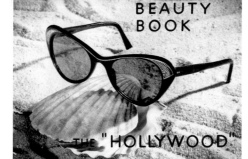

1

2

3

1
A skilled craftsman hand-polishes an Oliver Goldsmith frame.

2
In the 1950s Oliver Goldsmith was one of the first brands to appear regularly in women's fashion magazines.

3
Bamboo frames from the 1950s.

4
Cards, 1954.

5
Goo Goo, 1966.

6
Skoot, 1967.

4

business in 1960. He underwent three years' training in quality, elegance and comfort (QEC) before he was allowed to design his own frames by his father, who then largely handed over the reins in 1966, staying on as 'the old man'. The 1960s and 1970s were a golden age for the brand (the firm moved premises to Potters Bar, Hertfordshire, and stopped handmaking spectacles in 1972). During this period Oliver Goldsmith frames were selected by such celebrities as the actors Diana Dors, Michael Caine and Peter Sellers, the last of whom wore a Goldside style in 1974. Andrew Oliver Goldsmith designed a pair of metal granny glasses for John Lennon, which the star referred to affectionately as his 'Olivers'. Goldsmith also designed a notable pair of sunglasses for Audrey Hepburn for the film *Two for the Road* (1967). The film company had asked for them to be as large as possible, and the resulting Yu-Hu frame was so big that it needed specially moulded glass lenses; nevertheless it was later popular commercially, in white and candy-stripe.

Lord Snowdon, Princess Margaret's first husband, was Goldsmith's first royal client;

5

6

the peer is said to have arrived at the door at the same time as the comedian Arthur Askey, who denied he was with ''im'. Princess Grace of Monaco became a regular client after 'the old man' wrote to her, and he subsequently persuaded her to acquire a whole 'wardrobe' of glasses, such as Hope (*c.* 1963), a shallow oblong frame with wide aluminium sides – which she wore on the cover of *Look* magazine in 1969 – and Appo (1965), an unusual PRO design with a distinctive aluminium wrap-around brow-bar, which she wore to go skiing. Regular repeat visits to the Principality followed, to offer new frames.

British royal clients did not always provide such lavish patronage. In the 1970s Princess Margaret liked only one design, the polyoval, based on the UK's post-decimal fifty-pence coin; her frames, therefore, always had to be repaired or duplicated. Goldsmith was in contact with Lady Diana Spencer even before she married Prince Charles, but the brand won global fame from 1982, when the princess commissioned pieces to match her dresses; the most memorable were the Berwick, a white semi-aviator frame that she wore on the front cover of *Woman's Own* in 1986, and the red-and-white Nisha.

Oliver Goldsmith was also well known for its unusual frames, including black-and-white Op-Art examples. In the late 1970s the firm was asked by *Vogue* to design a set of sunglasses the likes of which had never been seen before, and it produced a famous polycarbonate pair with nose visor that had been moulded in France by Bollé; it did not sell in any great volume, but served the purpose of generating publicity. Many other

1
Goldside, from the 1970s.

2
Tutti, 1986. Thoroughly British, the Oliver Goldsmith brand has always sold well abroad, although, amazingly, the first foreign trade show it attended was Optica in Germany in 1982.

3, 4
The tennis-racket frame was designed by the second-generation Oliver Goldsmith in 1954. It was restyled by the third-generation Oliver Goldsmith in 1982.

1
Pyramid (1966), designed
specifically to go with a
Vidal Sassoon hairstyle.

2
Dogs, 1985.

3
The Y-Not (1968) featured
an imitation wood effect.

4, 5
Ducks, 1985.

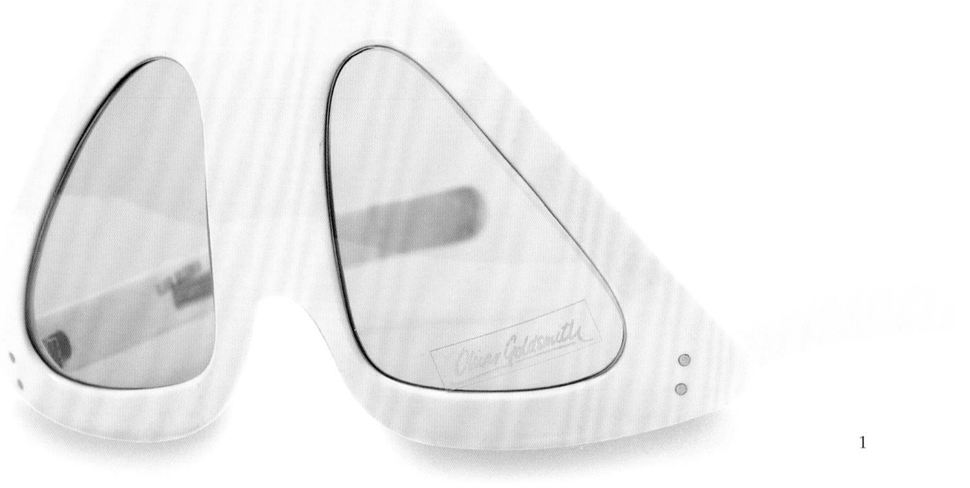

1

2

3

4

5

Goldsmith designs, such as the back-to-back dogs and the tennis rackets so beloved of contemporary collectors, should be viewed in a similar context.

In 1989 the company survived a public falling-out between Andrew Goldsmith and his brother Raymond. Separate new companies were formed: Oliver Goldsmith Eyewear, led by Andrew, moved to nearby Elstree; Oliver Goldsmith Sunglasses, led by Raymond, settled in Potters Bar. After Raymond's death in 1997 the sunglasses brand went into abeyance before being revived by his daughter, Claire Goldsmith, in 2004. Working exclusively in prescription eyewear, Andrew Goldsmith has had success selling the Oliver Goldsmith back-catalogue designs to Japan: he first supplied 18-carat solid-gold styles to the country in about 2001 through Mari Vision in Osaka, and relaunched the 1960s range there in 2006 (the current bestseller is the Vice Consul in shell). Today he sees himself as a 'traditional rebel', and his designs, regarded as outlandish when first introduced, are widely popular. Recognizing that people may not be able to change their spectacles as often as their outfits and may want to wear a frame over several years, he knows that a classic look can appeal. In his opinion, new designers cannot do retro in the way an old hand who was doing it the first time around can. Andrew Goldsmith now says that he likes to design for older people – to make them feel younger – and he was quoted in *Optometry Today* in May 2007 as saying that, these days, 'the stars for me are the general public'.

Harold Lloyd

(1893–1971) American film actor and producer, best known for his silent comedies

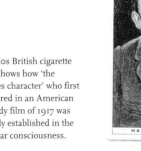

A 1920s British cigarette card shows how 'the glasses character' who first appeared in an American comedy film of 1917 was already established in the popular consciousness.

While Oliver Goldsmith was pioneering experimental frames in 1920s England, on the other side of the Atlantic a film star was the principal driving force. Harold Clayton Lloyd Sr was so very nearly just another American silent-movie actor, turning his hand to various comic characters in the 1910s; but in 1917, in the comedy feature *Over the Fence*, he put on a pair of empty rimmed spectacles and became 'the glasses character' for which he is now most famous. The spectacles supposedly made the character look like an everyday kind of guy – an unusual step to take, since at that time character was normally conveyed through exaggerated facial features and excessive make-up – allowing audiences to identify with Lloyd as they laughed along.

The renowned producer Hal Roach, who worked with Lloyd on many films, recalled that in 1917 the actor Earl Mohan had arrived at the studio wearing newly fashionable horn-rimmed spectacles, and that this might have been the origin of Lloyd's idea for his most famous prop. Lloyd himself often told another

story: that he had been inspired by a film featuring a go-getting bespectacled minister. The actor believed that the spectacles made his character attractive to women, both on screen and off.

Lloyd's glasses certainly spurred a growth in demand for spectacles across the United States, particularly among the young, who were perhaps persuaded that adopting eyewear could contribute towards an enhanced personality. Towards the end of his life Lloyd claimed to have 'felt bound in' until he put on the spectacles, after which, for the first time, he became 'free' – partly because when he took them off he could wallow in glorious real-life anonymity.

Lloyd's spectacles frames, of imitation tortoiseshell with curl sides, came in for a lot of punishment: in his films he scaled buildings and hung from clock faces, played American football and even fought in a boxing match while wearing them. The earliest films feature thinner rims than he would later use, but they look quite prominent because of the thickly caked cinematic make-up. The Optical Products Corporation

(OPC) frame supplier sent Lloyd six frames at a time, to ensure that he would never be without, and provided them free of charge, such was the favourable publicity. The rims were unglazed, as the studio lights would have reflected off the lenses, but their shadow is often visible on his whitened face. In *Movie Crazy* (1932) Lloyd gets his head stuck in a cage of birds and is actually pecked in the eye through his empty rim.

Lloyd's make-up box, which he left to his granddaughter's husband, contained several pairs of glasses supplied by the Reynolds Company of New York, including a glazed pair that he used for personal appearances (the actor was temporarily blinded in one eye in 1920 after a publicity shot with a supposedly fake bomb went explosively wrong). In later life Lloyd wore prescription spectacles, but the rims were a PRO shape.

An outline of Lloyd's screen spectacles was included in the Hollywood Walk of Fame in 1927, alongside his handprints, footprints and autograph, and his bespectacled image has appeared on all sorts of merchandise.

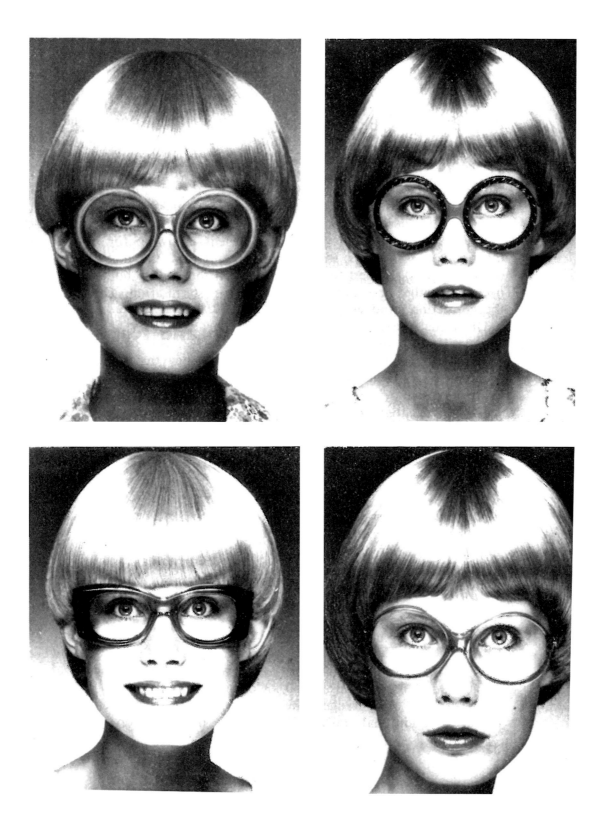

Algha | Mary Quant | Savile Row

'Algha', its five letters so often seen engraved beneath a nose bridge, was both a British brand and a London factory, and is now a company and, indeed, a brand again in certain countries. While the company structure has changed numerous times, the product range has stayed remarkably constant under its new name of Savile Row. Some 90 per cent of Algha's models have survived largely unchanged; for film companies, this has the benefit that they can buy authentic vintage styles that will nevertheless look new on screen. It is therefore possible to speak of cult styles, not merely a cult brand.

Max Wiseman (1878–1956) established the London optical business M. Wiseman & Co. in 1898, importing gold-filled frames in preference to the British-produced steel or solid-gold frames, but became interested in starting manufacture. His big move had to wait until 1932, when he bought the entire contents of a factory in Rathenow, Germany, and relocated it, staff and all, to a former printing works in Bow, east London. This became the Algha Works factory, and a counter-sinking machine from the 1920s is still in use there today. The name Algha was formed by a contraction of the words

for the first and last letters of the Greek alphabet, alpha and omega, giving rise to the slogan 'From beginning to end – a spectacle'. The first manager, Siegfried Sacki, turned an empty shell of a factory into a profitable concern within eight weeks. Wiseman repeated the feat in 1933, importing the entire contents of the Mantor frame factory from Rathenow, and opened a factory for synthetic shell frames, thus becoming completely independent of foreign supplies.

The Algha factory was one of the first to produce a catalogue of 'styled frames', in 1933, but after the National Health Service was established in 1948 the firm concentrated on manufacturing NHS frames. It was one of the two main suppliers to the NHS (the other was Merx Optical), producing 1.5 million frames a year in the firm's early 1960s heyday, and it was also strong in the Far East. Between 1965 and 1970 M. Wiseman & Co. underwent many changes, becoming first UK Wiseman, then United Kingdom Optical (UKO) B&L, and finally fully merging with UKO, bringing a new logo on to the Algha Works parapet.

New ideas were introduced at Algha in the 1970s, including the London Line frame

The Algha Works in Bow, east London.

Max Wiseman, who established the Algha factory in 1932. Wiseman was instrumental in founding the Association of Wholesale and Manufacturing Opticians, forerunner of today's Federation of Manufacturing Opticians.

OPPOSITE
Original advertising by Wiseman for the first Mary Quant range, 1973.

collection and a sunglasses range produced by Mary Quant, the first British fashion designer to lend her name to a range of sunglasses. Quant had gained notoriety in 1955 on opening her 'anti-establishment' shop Bazaar on London's King's Road. Such amateur boutiques seized the fashion lead from department stores, and London was regarded as particularly experimental in this respect. Quant's second shop, designed by Terence Conran, opened in 1957. By the time Max Wiseman's son Frank (1912–1995) came knocking on her door in the early 1970s, she had introduced the miniskirt, established a flourishing export business with the United States, received an OBE and published an autobiography, *Quant by Quant* (1966), and was about to be the object of a retrospective exhibition at the Museum of London (1973).

So although at first glance Wiseman and Quant's collaboration might have seemed an unlikely one, Wiseman was not exactly taking a risk, as approaching upcoming young talent might have been. The fact that the firm wanted to diversify, when there was as yet no perceived threat to the market for NHS glasses, is noteworthy in itself. With more than forty years of manufacturing behind his firm, Wiseman had the factories and the in-house skills but needed to project a new image, and Quant was by now an established name. The first Mary Quant range was launched at London's Savoy Hotel in 1973. Quant not only designed the range in its entirety but also selected the colours and specified the precise materials. (Although Quant is commonly associated

The ◉ MARY QUANT Fashion Range

MODEL No.	STYLE	COLOUR CODE	DATUM EYESIZE	DBL's
MQ 07		C. Rosy D. Delphinium L. Hyacinth R. Amaryllis	52 54	18, 20 18, 20
MQ 08		CC. Chestnut DD. Evening Glow Q. Love in Bloom L. Hyacinth	52 54	16, 18 16, 18
MQ 09		Z. Candytuft AA. Sweet Harmony BB. Anemone	52 54	16, 18 16, 18
MQ 10		W. Opal Brown X. Opal Blue	52 54	18, 20 18, 20
MQ 11		R. Amaryllis T. Harlequin U. Heather V. Blue Moon	50 52	18, 20 18, 20
MQ 12		R. Amaryllis T. Harlequin U. Heather Y. Sepia	50 52	18, 20 18, 20

with black and white, her first eyewear range most frequently survives in its black and brown versions.)

Some opticians were horrified at the direction their trusted manufacturing supplier was taking. In a letter published in the *Ophthalmic Optician* in March 1973, W.H. Todd of Blackpool wrote: 'The demand for these frames is expected to be heavy. I trust that there are opticians like myself who will boycott the frames and make the demand less heavy than expected.' The six models in the Mary Quant range had no fancy names, as that would have detracted from the novelty of the brand name itself; instead, each model was identified simply on the inner sides with the numbers 01 to 06. Marketing was carried out in both the British and the mainland continental markets, the frames being presented at such fairs as the Intercontinental Optical Fair in Brussels in 1973. According to reports at the time, special attention had been paid to the strength of the joints, the quality of the general finish and the fit – but herein lay the rub: this first range of Mary Quant sunglasses frequently

1, 2
Mary Quant 05 with daisy logo, 1973.

3
Catalogue for the second Mary Quant range, *c.* 1974.

4, 5
Savile Row Panto Beaufort OSRC5, 1990s.

Mary Quant 01 model, 1973. All the frames in the Mary Quant range featured pinless joints and sides that matched their fronts. No rivet heads or plates were permitted to show – an unusual step for its time.

A Savile Row model from the late twentieth century, with octagonal rims and associated packaging.

An unidentified Savile Row model with beautifully striped ends.

didn't fit well. They sold well, but customers were often left dissatisfied. Professional opponents of fashion eyewear must have been secretly delighted.

A second Mary Quant range was launched the following year, at London's Grosvenor House Hotel; it was afforded the title of a sub-collection, the Grosvenor Collection. Quant and Wiseman stood together to publicize the new range, but what went unspoken was that this time Quant had had less input. Traditional skilled spectacle makers had instead taken control. The six new models carried on the numerical sequence, from 07 to 12. Though of better quality, they are less collectible than frames 01–06, from the first range.

In 1986 UKO and the Algha Works were purchased by American Optical (AO; p. 23), and further fashion-led initiatives were tried; for a period from 1987, UKO was appointed distributor for French eyewear designer Alain Mikli (p. 135). The Savile Row range was launched in 1988 as a niche product, offering traditional quality and style, all handmade and all British. As a brand name, Savile Row was intended to be a direct replacement of Algha, because the latter was too closely associated with the NHS to be considered commercial. AO spread the new brand further, especially to the United States and Australia; the Algha Works also produced a number of own-brand gold frames for such companies as Kirk Originals (p. 39) and Boots Opticians.

By 1996 AO had just two frame plants, at the Algha Works and in Southbridge, Massachusetts (which produced Skymaster military frames), and was concentrating on

Savile Row M1 half-eye,
late twentieth century.

Savile Row Gallery 76,
late twentieth century.

Savile Row Warwick Silver
of 2001, as worn by Daniel
Radcliffe in the film
*Harry Potter and the
Philosopher's Stone*, released
the same year.

Rolled-gold joints being soldered in the traditional manner at Algha Works in 2010, for a Savile Row item.

its core business of lenses. Peter Viner, a consultant who had worked for UKO for several years, established Algha Group Ltd, and returned Algha to being a family business, with Philip Birkenstein from Progress Products (whose father developed Xylonite plastic Windsor covers for metal rims) as senior partner. Initially the firm benefited from very good American orders, supplying 250 handmade frames a month to one client alone, and all went well until it lost its order from Boots. This started a domino effect, and soon the company was struggling. In 2002 Viner bought out Birkenstein (whose core business switched to Theo Fabergé).

Back in the UKO days Viner had pioneered the use of Cellidor (a very hard plastic), being one of only two European frame makers to do so. Clear granules were melted down, given a base colour and then injection-moulded. This resulted in a lighter, more flexible material than sheet acetate, with a wider variety of colours. The high-quality hinges included a locking nylon washer that made the screw self-lock, preventing loose sides and loss of screws. The Algha Group bought Kirk Originals'

machinery, as well as its stocks of Optiroid plastic, when that company abandoned its Clacton-on-Sea factory in 2001. For a while there was a flourishing trade in supplying handmade plastic frames to Denmark, but in the face of lost orders the company concentrated once more on classic metal frames.

The PRO rim shape is now the Savile Row brand's core business, and the old NHS 722 is still made, although now styled 'Executive'. Up to 80 per cent of production is exported; recently markets have included Australia, Belgium and Vietnam. This brand had only ever been made in precious metals, such as 24-carat gold (£37 per gram at the time of writing) or rhodium (£135 per gram), but 'gunmetal' is to be introduced, using ruthenium. It is an interesting lesson that in eyewear, 'gold' is not always the most expensive material! A new Algha line that is not gold-filled but gold-plated (or rhodium-plated) is now offered to a limited market, and is not generally sold to Britain but rather to such countries as the emerging market of Bangladesh. The intention is never to dilute the Savile Row brand.

John Lennon

*(1940–1980) English musician
and singer-songwriter, a founding
member of The Beatles*

John Lennon in about 1970.
His fondness for round
frames has led to a market
in 'John Lennon type'
models. Lennon often wore
Algha frames, including
some of identical design
to the model subsequently
rebranded as Saville Row
Panto 45 frame, with cable
curl sides and yellow lenses
(opposite), and the Warwick
eyeglasses in rhodium.

Imagine if there had been no Beatles ... What would we have called all those round metal spectacles if John Lennon had not lived? Lennon abandoned spectacles in childhood and started wearing them regularly again only in the mid-1960s, initially just during rehearsals (he wore contact lenses at other times). According to one account, the round-eye style was given to him in preparation for his role as Private Gripweed in the film *How I Won the War* (1967), and in between filming sessions he couldn't be bothered to take them off.

In fact Lennon's eyewear was considerably more diverse than the generic Windsor type often afforded his name. Vintage Shuron and Ray-Ban frames can frequently be seen for sale today described as 'John Lennon type' – not always with much justification. Lennon's frames were often more PRO-shaped than round and had a variety of bridge styles, although at various

times he certainly did wear the National Health Service PRO model known as 422CJ ('CJ' standing for 'centre joints'), which had an upwardly crested pad bridge and in which to the untrained eye the rims look broadly round. Far from fashionable in its day, the 422 was a subsidized NHS range that has now developed retro appeal only because it has been discontinued.

In 1966 The Beatles donated twelve pairs of various spectacles to the British and Overseas Optical Mission; one of these, a gold-rimmed pair of Lennon's with a W-bridge and curl sides, has what are, emphatically, oval eyes – although this did not stop them from being described as typically round when they were first exhibited to the public in 2009 at London's Millennium Dome.

Examples of 'John Lennon glasses' (the phrase has been traced back to a piece by Judith Viorst in *New York Magazine* of April 1969) with tinted lenses, also known in

the late 1960s as 'teashades', were popular with rock stars of the era, perhaps because they were thought to mask the traces of marijuana abuse. Today they are perhaps most associated with Ozzy Osbourne. An interview Lennon gave to *Rolling Stone* magazine the week before he was murdered (in December 1980) confirms, however, that he had stopped wearing 'John Lennon glasses' in 1973.

The blood-spattered plastic-rimmed pair he was wearing when he was shot was used by his wife, Yoko Ono, as a cover image on her album *Season of Glass* in 1981, and original prints of this photograph are now valuable collectors' items in themselves, one having sold for almost £9000 in 2002.

Lennon was responsible for contributing to the interest in his spectacles by giving away examples of his eyewear. One of these 'gifts', a complete pair of gold-plated spectacles, sold at Sotheby's auctioneers in 1987 for what now seems to be a bargain £5844. In 1971

Lennon called on optometrist Hermann Dungs in San Rafael, California, bought two pairs of spectacles and presented him with his old pair's lenses, which he said were 'all scratched up'. The practice was raided by thieves in 2008, but the burglars missed the lenses because they had been taken off display and left in a soap tray in the bathroom.

Sometimes Lennon even autographed the lenses. He did so on a plain wire pair of spectacles that was presented to Junishi Yore, a Japanese translator for Nippon TV, in 1966, and these came up for an online auction in 2007, but minus their orange-tinted lenses; on hearing of his friend's murder, Yore had broken them as part of a traditional Japanese ritual to release the soul of the departed. The spectacles are thought to have fetched in excess of £1 million.

In his later career, when he lived in New York, Lennon wore aviator-style rims and clip-over sunglasses. A range

inspired by John Lennon's and Yoko Ono's spectacles of the 1970s, officially endorsed by the Lennon estate, was offered by J.L. Optical in Britain in 1998 and by Ambassador Eyewear in the United States in 2000. Potential stockists were encouraged to 'put your business on an upbeat note'. A further range of sunglasses in nickel silver was launched in Britain in tribute to Lennon in 2009 by i-Sunglasses.

The cult of 'John Lennon glasses' goes beyond actual spectacles: in the John Lennon Park in Havana, Cuba, there is a statue of him seated on a bench, and fans are forever stealing the removable spectacles, so these are consequently removed whenever a guard cannot be present; and at Liverpool airport in 2007, one fan ripped off a cast-bronze pair that was an integral part of Lennon's statue there.

Polaroid

Historically, most frames inscribed 'Polaroid' merely incorporated Polaroid lenses, and the frames themselves may have been unremarkable. The Polaroid Corporation did not actually manufacture any sunglasses until 1976. Prior to that date, frames for this all-American brand were produced under licence by other companies, many of which were based outside the United States.

In 1926, while walking along New York City's Broadway, a young man named Edwin Herbert Land (1909–1991) noted the glare of illuminated signs and car headlights. Working first at Columbia University laboratory (although he was not a student there) and later at Harvard University in Cambridge, Massachusetts (where he was registered for one year), this prodigy developed a synthetic sheet polariser and in 1929 filed a patent application to protect it commercially. The product, known at first as the J-Sheet, incorporated small, mechanically stretched needle-shaped crystals; colleagues thought of naming it 'Epibolipol', but Land settled on the catchier 'Polaroid'. With Harvard physics lecturer George Wheelwright III he set up a manufacturing laboratory in the nearby town of Wellesley Hills, and in 1932 he announced publicly the first synthetic material to polarise light. Land had intended it for use on car headlights but was prevented from pursuing this by prior patents, so its first application was for Polascreen camera filters for Eastman Kodak in 1934.

The Land-Wheelwright laboratory had already been experimenting with the film on sunglass lenses, and its second contract, in 1935, was with American Optical (AO; p. 23) for 'Polaroid Day Glasses'. The deal was sealed after Land rented a room in Boston's Copley Plaza Hotel and placed a fish tank in front of a brightly lit window, and then handed AO executives some filter film as they entered the room so that they could see the fish more clearly in the glare. Polaroid Day Glasses were launched in the United States in December 1936, and American Optical had a dedicated Polaroid sunglasses division from after the Second World War until 1975. Land established the Polaroid Corporation in 1937 and subsequently negotiated a further licensing agreement with Bausch & Lomb, makers of Ray-Ban sunglasses (p. 67) – so, remarkably, the two greatest rivals in American optical manufacturing were both

Edwin Land (facing the camera) developed the Polaroid light polariser in the late 1920s. He stepped down as the corporation's president in 1975 and as CEO in 1980, but remained chairman of the board until 1982. During the course of his life Land held more American patents than anyone else other than Thomas Edison.

A trade-show notice of 1937 from the British subsidiary of American Optical, which first licensed Polaroid for use in lenses. The Polaroid trademark and logo of intersecting polarised discs was devised in 1935 but was not used here.

OPPOSITE
A French advertisement for Polaroid, 1977.

Polaroid advertising from Great Britain, 1976 (above, left), and Australia, 1956 (above, right).

Scottish-made Polaroid 8222 (post-1962) in a library frame style.

Model 4116 (mid- to late twentieth century) with branded vinyl case and test filter tag.

producing Polaroid sunglasses. Sunglasses (or sunglass lenses) therefore represent the corporation's first substantial commercial market, and in 1939 more than a million finished pairs were sold.

In the late 1940s, concurrently with the launch of the corporation's one-step photography system, Polaroid technicians developed scratch-resistant sunglass lenses and the stage was set for expansion. Polaroid first set up a British subsidiary in 1962 (sales had previously been handled by Johnsons of Hendon); manufacturing of sunglasses commenced at a factory in Scotland's Vale of Leven, near Loch Lomond, where it continues to the present day. In 1963 an advert for the prescription house Newbold & Co proclaimed that Polaroids were 'supplied exclusively by opticians' and that it had 'ample stocks of the full range'. There were various other suppliers, all of whom would order Polaroids by the box for one-third off the price, but this resulted in lots of stock being left over at the end of the season, and over time Polaroid began to lose its distribution. When the firm of Crofton & Blyth offered opticians a 25 per cent discount for single frames, the other distribution houses stopped buying whole sets.

In the 1960s many Polaroids were not particularly well made, and were certainly not up to ophthalmic standards. The better ones had laminated lenses. The 1967 sunglass collection, promoted in Britain at 50 shillings a pair, could be worn by both men and women; there was also a 33-shilling option for children. Sunglass Model 700 was available in black only, but in the *Ophthalmic Optician* its library style was said to be 'following one of the most predominant current fashion trends in presenting a large TV eye-shape'. (This style was also referred to as a 'picture frame'.) In 1969 Polaroid introduced an aviator style in Britain. The prominent lecturer and writer on optical matters Jack Davey (1924–2001) wrote in February 1969 in the *Ophthalmic Optician* that this was encouraging, as his own Polaroid sun spectacles were now 'back in fashion after a decade of obsolescence'.

The 1970s were a happier period for Polaroid. In 1975, in what was then an innovative promotion, UK stockists offered customers the chance to win a holiday to Jamaica. Product quality was now considered to be high again; the Lookers 1979 range, with a greater number of metal frames than plastic ones, represented 'the latest move by Polaroid to improve their fashion image to the level of their quality image', according to the *Ophthalmic Optician*. The 1982 range even included a leopard-skin print and tiger stripes – the 'skinny look'. At around the same time it was reported that the market for polarised sunglasses among motorists had increased because, thanks to the decreasing use of heat-toughened glass in car windscreens, fewer stresses showed up through polarised lenses.

By 1996 Polaroid was the market leader in Europe for polarised sunglasses, but in 2001 the parent company had to file for bankruptcy. After a long period of disruption Polaroid became part of the StyleMark Group, and in 2009 a new international company, Polaroid Eyewear, headquartered in Switzerland, emerged; the current portfolio also includes the Disney, Hello Kitty, Revlon and Sunmate brands.

Model 3201, yellow metal with a high stepped bridge (mid- to late twentieth century).

British Polaroid clip-overs from the 1970s, sold originally for £4.95.

A women's laminated acetate frame, 1960s.

Model 8529 F (early 1990s), of Italian design.

Ray-Ban

The American firm Bausch & Lomb Optical was the first to market sunglasses under a brand name, beating earlier producer Ratti's Persol (p. 45) by one year. Since it was registered in 1937 the Ray-Ban brand has represented high-quality but affordable simplicity resulting from its origins making sunglasses for military pilots. This has led to the brand being described as 'attainable fashion'.

Bausch & Lomb, which had been primarily a lens manufacturer, entered the spectacles frame-making business properly in 1922 when it bought the frame manufacturer Stevens & Company and moved production to Rochester, New York. In about 1930 Lt MacReady of the US Army Air Corps commissioned the firm to make lenses that would protect pilots' eyes from glare at high altitude. The resulting goggles, which went beyond his specifications, remained standard issue until 1941. 'Ray-Ban Pilots Glasses' were the first to be launched as a brand-name article, and were issued free to pilots while being offered for sale to the public. In 1936 the company took a bold step in producing a plastic frame with prescription-quality lenses; these 'anti-glare goggles' sold for $3.75 (as opposed to the

'To greater vision through optical science'. This medallion, which featured in a Bausch & Lomb catalogue of 1942, shows that the firm stressed the properties of its lenses.

Bausch & Lomb Ful-Vue goggles of the 1950s, incorporating Ray-Ban lenses.

The Gayest Thing in Sun Glasses

Ray-Ban FUN Glasses MADE BY BAUSCH & LOMB

Glamour Eyes for style-conscious patients! Bold, bright colors in this saucy (but ophthalmically correct) Zyl shape. Exciting news is the Ray-Ban Fun Glass, the style-challenger that offers the additional advantage of *safe, scientific glare protection* famous in genuine Ray-Ban Sun Glasses. In plano, or for Ray-Ban lenses on prescription.

Ray-Ban frame shapes and colours were emphasized in marketing material from an early date, as in this example from 1948.

OPPOSITE
Dan Aykroyd and John Belushi wearing Ray-Ban Wayfarers in *The Blues Brothers* (1980).

Ray Stegman (right) designed the original Ray-Ban Wayfarer in the early 1950s.

Aviator style from 1953.

Wayfarer in imitation shell with robust four-charnier joint, probably 1980s.

usual 25 cents for sunglasses). The name 'Anti-Glare' being too general to be offered legal protection, the brand was registered in 1937 as Ray-Ban – it did what the name suggested. The oversized Aviator sunglass frame was born, featuring a dark tinted lens of finely ground optical glass with a neutral grey filter capable of absorbing 80 per cent of transmitted light while still allowing accurate colour recognition.

The UK launch of Ray-Ban sunglasses was announced in *The Optician* in August 1938. The article's author, who describes himself as initially sceptical about sunglasses, states that behind Ray-Ban glass 'one experiences a coolness only to be described as delicious' (this is apparently one of the first references to the word 'cool' used with regard to eyewear). All production of the Aviator between 1942 and 1945 went towards the war effort: although Ray-Bans were no longer standard issue for the US Army Air Corps, and although military pilots seem to have preferred the rival range by American Optical (p. 23), Aviators were favoured by naval pilots. General Douglas MacArthur wore them all through the war, and later in Korea. The sunglasses were valuable items during both conflicts, and anecdotal reports suggest that they were used as barter in South-east Asia. Aviators from the Classic Metals series featured prominently in the Tom Cruise film *Top Gun* (1986), and in 1985 the Aviator received an award from the Council of Fashion Designers of America.

In 1952 Ray Stegman, a Ray-Ban designer, designed the Wayfarer, which, with its slightly curving upper rims, has become the all-time classic Ray-Ban frame. Some claim that it is the bestselling style in history, and it has been worn across the decades, for example by Marilyn Monroe in the late 1950s and by Don Johnson in the 1980s television series *Miami Vice*. It had been discontinued, but was reintroduced, not for the only time, in 1983. Leather Wayfarers were promoted as a premium line in about 1989, while such other styles as the Laramie and the Meteor were reminiscent of the Wayfarer but more upswept. In 1993 Bausch & Lomb issued a fortieth-anniversary replica edition of the original Wayfarer featuring its RB-3 green lens and a tortoiseshell frame. Other variations have included the Wayfarer Street Neat mosaic collection, featuring five colour combinations, and the feminine Innerview of 1994. In 1996 Aaron Markovitz, Ray-Ban's vice president of worldwide marketing and design, commented that the Wayfarer identity was so strong that the model kept going, whereas other successful Ray-Ban sunglasses were allowed to sell out without being continued.

In Britain (where a factory was opened in 1958), in 1980 some 85 per cent of Ray-Bans were sold through department stores, but extensive promotion meant that by 1990 90 per cent were sold through opticians,

Easy Rider

American road movie (1969), directed by Dennis Hopper; starring Peter Fonda and Dennis Hopper

Peter Fonda wearing Ray-Bans from 1968 in *Easy Rider*.

A low-budget road movie of motorcycles, sex and drugs, *Easy Rider* starred Peter Fonda (who also produced and co-wrote) and Dennis Hopper (who also directed). It became a cult counterculture film, but it also proved that sunglasses don't assist your vision, since, as the marketing tag went, behind those glasses, 'A man went looking for America. And couldn't find it anywhere.'

Fonda and Hopper play two young men from Los Angeles who set off on chopper motorcycles to attend Mardi Gras in New Orleans. Even before the opening titles roll, the viewer has been treated to several close-up shots of eyewear. In Mexico a pair of Ray-Ban Olympian I De Luxe with a relatively light tint nestles on Fonda's nose as he snorts the cocaine he will shortly be selling in order to finance the adventure. The action cuts to Los Angeles airport, where the drug 'connection' (played by music producer and songwriter Phil Spector) sports a remarkable Ray-Ban Shooter frame with an open ring-shaped bridge and amber-tinted lenses, and his bodyguard (Mac Mashourian, Spector's real-life bodyguard) models a fine pair of plastic wraparound shades.

The principal characters may call each other 'dude', but it is important not to mistake their look as unambiguously cool. By the time *Easy Rider* was released the Summer of Love was over. Far from attracting the admiring glances of their countrymen, the two main characters project a universally off-putting image: they are refused entry even to second-rate motels; the adolescent girls in a small-town café pay them curious attention, but the waiting staff do not offer them service; they are attacked in their sleeping bags by hostile locals; and at one point beside a camp fire Fonda is forced to remove his spectacles as smoke gets in his eyes – even nature is against them! The characters are trapped in the end of the 1960s and destined never to see the 1970s: in the final scene the pair are killed by poachers.

The Blues Brothers

American musical comedy film (1980), directed by John Landis; starring John Belushi and Dan Aykroyd

Pin badges celebrating the film *The Blues Brothers*.

'It's 106 miles to Chicago, we've got a full tank of gas, half a pack of cigarettes, it's dark, and we're wearing sunglasses' – so says the motor fanatic and veteran musician Elwood Blues (played by Dan Aykroyd) in the cult musical comedy *The Blues Brothers* just before the final climactic car chase. The opening scene also features sunglasses, as newly released convict Jake Blues (John Belushi) passes through the prison stores to recover his shades, the only item in his wardrobe that isn't strictly black.

Thereafter he and his brother find it practically impossible to shed their Ray-Ban Wayfarer I frames: they wear them indoors as well as out, in the sauna and while performing multiple somersaults down a church aisle; they retain them when the nun at their former orphanage asks them to come forwards so she can see their faces; and when their hotel is blown up around them, and a telephone box in which they are making a call is sent rocketing skywards, their sunglasses are scarcely moved. They are, after all, 'on a mission from God' to raise money to save an orphanage.

These lovable rogues made unlikely cult figures. The two characters' overall look was based on 1950s album covers of such artists as John Lee Hooker, but the sunglasses were an addition by Aykroyd and Belushi for the Blues Brothers' first appearance, on the American television series *Saturday Night Live* in 1978; the duo had also released a bestselling album before the film was shown in cinemas. Not for nothing does a line in the film state that they are wearing the same suits they wore three years ago. These suits may have been self-consciously old-fashioned, but the look spurred a huge increase in demand for Wayfarers.

who could now obtain the brand only direct from the parent company, not from wholesalers. A 1980s model, the Drifter, retailed for £55 in black or tortoiseshell (£59 with coloured upper rim). In 1987 the Ray-Ban Rx was the brand's first offering to the prescription market, featuring a deeper rim groove to take a wide range of optical lenses. This was promoted – without a hint of irony – as making the Ray-Ban look 'accessible to spectacle wearers'.

The first Ray-Ban collection to be produced exclusively for the non-American market was the Premier Traditionals collection of 1990, based on styles of the 1930s and 1940s and made of ebony or tortoiseshell with 24-carat gold-plated fittings and filigree bridges, and fitted with the original grey-green G15 lenses. In 1991 French superstar eyewear designer Alain Mikli (p. 135) designed the Onyx collection for Ray-Ban.

In 1992 Bausch & Lomb invested $28 million in a new Ray-Ban manufacturing facility in Waterford, Ireland, and the firm was also the official worldwide sunglasses sponsor at the Barcelona Olympics. In 1998 some 10 million pairs of Ray-Bans were sold; the brand was responsible for 30 per cent of Bausch & Lomb's entire sales, and it outsold competitor brands by a ratio of 4 to 1. But the firm's decision to concentrate on lenses rather than frames meant that in 1999 Ray-Ban was sold to the Italian Luxottica Group, along with the Killer Loop, Revo and Arnette brands.

1
A British advertisement from 1972.

2
A shop display in Germany in 2010 shows the variety of colours and patterns that Ray-Ban has developed since becoming part of the Luxottica Group's portfolio in 1999.

3
This Drifter frame was probably manufactured in the 1950s or 1960s. The style reappeared in the 1980s.

4
A prominent proclamation of Ray-Ban's 'Never Hide' brand promotion of 2010, at the Galeries Lafayette department store in Paris.

5
Wayfarer II, produced to mark the 1992 Barcelona Olympics.

3

4

5

Pierre Marly

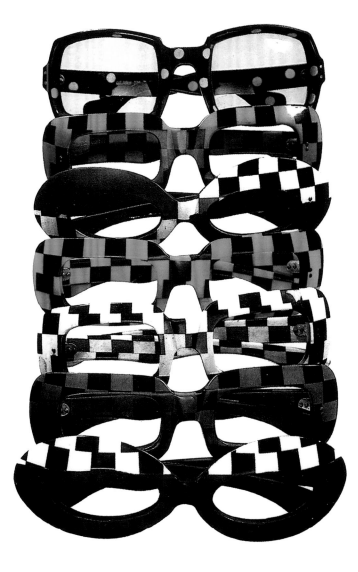

Pierre Marly, photographed in the 1960s.

Polka-dot and chequered pattern frames, *c.* 1965–75.

Many fashion eyewear brands have been keen to publicize their appeal to celebrity clients, but French optician Pierre Marly actually met all of his, and developed relationships with them akin to being a close adviser or stylist. Throughout the second half of the twentieth century they came to his shop in Paris to peruse frames of his own design; he dispensed their spectacles in person and then they signed his visitors' book, thereby joining an elite club.

Born in 1915, Marly was apprenticed to an optician-photographer in his home town of Arpajon, south of Paris, where he learned to glaze spectacles. He was then taken on as a salesman by the well-known optical firm of Les Frères Lissac, serving in various shops before progressing to the Parisian department store La Samaritaine. Recognized early on for his talent, Marly was taken under the wing of the company founder, Georges Lissac, and rose to become successively director of the workshop, director of supplies, technical director and finally managing director.

While working for Lissac, Marly persuaded the company to make spectacle frames, not just sell them, and became head

OPPOSITE
These tennis-racket frames from 1957 were so characteristic of Marly's work and style that he called them, simply, Pierre Marly.

The asymmetrical pattern of this frame, issued *c.* 1955–65, was compared to a Harlequin costume.

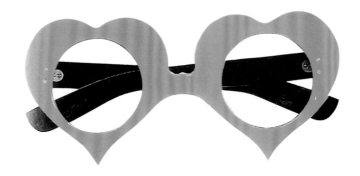

Heart-shaped frame, *c.* 1965–75.

Caricature of Pierre Marly by Siné (Maurice Sinet), 1960s.

By the 1960s Marly himself had attained high celebrity status. The French caricaturist Siné produced a cartoon of him as *le roi des opticiens* (king of opticians) in the manner of a playing card, and also drew a caricature in the visitors' book in which he described Marly as 'the optician who dresses the eyes of the stars'. This visitors' book, or 'Golden Book' as it is known in the family, is preserved to this day in the successor practice on Paris's rue François 1er. Given the almost ubiquitous use in the optical and fashion press of the phrase 'Jackie O glasses', it is interesting to note that Jackie Kennedy Onassis came here for her spectacles; the many others from show business and positions of high office who bought Marly eyewear include the French statesman's wife Claude Pompidou, the filmmaker François Truffaut, Maria Callas, Audrey Hepburn, Ursula Andress, Alec Guinness, Brigitte Bardot, Nana Mouskouri, Glenn Ford, Catherine Deneuve, Sammy Davis Jr and Charles Aznavour.

In 1967 the actress Jeanne Moreau wrote a letter (which is pasted into the book) apologizing for late payment because she had been moving house. An ageing Marlene Dietrich came through the door in 1970. It was not uncommon for these people to pen a complimentary message to their optician. Jane Fonda, for example, wrote 'Thanks for the marvellous glasses', and Madonna, who visited the shop in 1995, wrote 'Now I can see clearly.' Taking their lead from Siné, other customers were inspired to produce their own works of instant art in the Golden Book: the actor Sean Flynn (son of Errol) drew an elephant's bottom in 1964; in about 1969–70 the secretary of state Philippe

of its new venture, the Société industrielle de lunetterie (SIL), which specialized in the manufacture of plastic frames and lenses, and launched the Amor and Nylor frames. Finally, having passed his French optician's diploma in 1948, he embarked on his destined career as a 'designer', a word not commonly used in relation to eyewear at the time.

Marly opened his own business in Melun, south-east of Paris, that year and soon opened four more branches in Paris itself, including one on the upmarket avenue Mozart, to which all the most glamorous people flocked. When Hollywood actress Grace Kelly came to France in 1955 (just prior to meeting her future husband, Prince Rainier of Monaco), she was wearing a Pierre Marly frame.

Dechartre drew a self-caricature with umbrella and ministerial briefcase; Karl Lagerfeld drew a picture in 1991 (when he had not yet made his own name in spectacle design); and in 1992 the composer Vangelis drew a picture of a classical Greek bust with laurel wreath and spectacles – in other words, he was judging Marly to be worthy of the highest accolade.

While many of these celebrities bought good-quality but nevertheless conventionally styled frames, the business was known for its flamboyant designs. The Plume au Vent ('windblown feather') design lasted for several decades and was provided in several different versions, including some encrusted with jewels. There is something very theatrical about many of the designs, such as the 1960s Panoramic model, which has been compared to a highwayman's mask, and the popular 1970s Harlequinade, and they can be regarded as pieces of costume. Some Marly frames, such as the Bicycle frame of 1970, were created primarily for display and would have been impractical to wear. Marly also designed for the Courrèges fashion house, including a pair that can be described only as Eskimo goggles.

Marly's inspiration was drawn from his extensive knowledge, built up through collecting ophthalmic antiques; he advertised widely his interest in acquiring oddities from around the world to display in his private museum, and promoted them in his book *Spectacles and Spyglasses* (1988). Maybe the last word should go to actress Geraldine Chaplin, for whom Pierre Marly produced, as she wrote in his Golden Book, quite simply *'les plus belles lunettes du monde!'*

Margaret Dowaliby

(born 1924) American optometrist, pioneer promoter of cosmetic and fashion eyewear

Margaret Dowaliby in the 1960s. Below, an Art-Craft frame in anodised aluminium (*c.* 1960) of the type she encouraged in her articles for the American optometry profession.

The cosmetic effect of eyewear and the 'glamorous new world' it ushered in was proclaimed by the American optometrist Dr Margaret Dowaliby. She introduced formal courses on the subject at the Los Angeles College of Optometry (now Southern California College of Optometry) in the late 1940s, and organized in conjunction with a top modelling agency a pioneering one-hour fashion show (open only to members of the optometric profession) that was held in a Beverly Hills hotel.

For Dowaliby the subject was about the elegance of jewels, the loveliness of precious metals, the smartness of styled line and the excitement of colour, even if green frames – which she recommended – were still too 'new' to enjoy widespread use. It was also about psychology, with, for example, an unprecedented importance placed on dispensing for children who wanted to ape their parents or elder siblings. Dowaliby was

also aware of the particular practicalities of fitting spectacle frames to patients who had undergone cosmetic facial surgery, especially to the nose.

In 1961 Dowaliby published the book *Modern Eyewear: Fashion and Cosmetic Dispensing*, drawn from a series of articles that had first appeared in the *Optometric Weekly* professional journal and illustrated with diagrams and fashion photographs from such suppliers as Art-Craft. Dowaliby's unique background, which included training from fashion experts and time instructing on charm and personal grooming at the Los Angeles Trade Technical Junior College, prepared her to write on such topics as facial characteristics, frame weight (*i.e.* thickness of material) and the role of eyewear as an essential part of a patient's total dress.

Dowaliby showed how training of the optometrist in this area grew out of the curriculum for mechanical

optics, originally in necessary response to the challenge of glazing newer-style frames. In *Modern Eyewear*, she argued that the time had come for consumers, especially women, to possess 'a wardrobe of glasses' to vary with the seasons or to wear 'after-five', and that the lessons understood by the manufacturers of eye make-up should be applied to classic or 'conventional' eyewear, as distinct from 'fad' frames that broke all the rules but also had a value in revitalizing market interest.

'Looking at a person wearing glasses,' Dowaliby wrote in her book, 'one should receive the impression that the frame was designed specifically for the wearer.' One reviewer commented in the December 1961 issue of the *Ophthalmic Optician*: 'Frivolous as it may appear, cosmetic dispensing and eyewear styling have come to be accepted as part of the optometrist's complement of knowledge in this field.'

Carrera | Carrera Porsche Design | Porsche Design

The Porsche Design brand is a classic example of how various eyewear companies – in particular two established and distinguished frame manufacturers, Wilhelm Anger in Austria and Rodenstock in Germany – took a new direction after contracting to take an additional brand into their portfolios.

In 1950 the Mexican government celebrated the completion of its section of the Pan-American Highway by sponsoring a five-day car race. The legendary Carrera Panamericana ran just five times (1950–54), in which time it achieved one of the highest mortality rates of any race in history. Nevertheless, it won wider fame thanks to the involvement of such important racing drivers as the Argentinian Juan Manuel Fangio, and was influential in the history of various motor brands, notably Porsche, which won the small sports car class in 1953. That same year Wilhelm Anger (see Viennaline/Serge Kirchhofer, p. 87) secured the use of the Carrera name for a range of ski goggles. The brand would grow into one of the foremost sports eyewear labels, notable from the 1970s for such innovations as the use of interchangeable lenses. The Carrera story really moves up a gear

in 1977, with the opening of a new sports sunglasses factory in Traun, Austria. The Carrera name would enjoy particular prominence in the United States because a company of that name would also be the American distributor for the Optyl brands of Christian Dior (p. 109), Hugo Boss, Terri Brogan, Alfred Dunhill, Sunjet and Christian Lacroix.

In 1979 Carrera collaborated with the automotive designer Ferdinand Alexander Porsche to produce its famed Carrera Porsche Design eyewear collection. Porsche had set up a design studio in 1972 for products other than cars, making, among other things, a matt-black chronograph and a compass watch in titanium, and first designed eyewear in association with the

Alpine ski racer Karl Schranz wearing a Carrera mask in the 1960s.

OPPOSITE
Stylish black-and-white marketing imagery for Carrera Porsche Design, 1985.

Sunjet sunglasses by Carrera. The side visors on this particular model, the funky 5249 (1990s), resemble Venetian blinds.

Die Gussfassung (the Cast Frame), Carrera Porsche Design, 1985.

The Carrera 5485 (1980s), a one-piece shield.

Carrera 5543 sports glasses from the 1990s.

A model from the Carrera Boeing range, designed in collaboration with the aeronautical manufacturer in 1986.

Italian firm Luxottica in 1978. The Carrera Porsche Design range included flat-folding models, wraparound goggles and titanium frames, available from around 1981. That year Carrera began producing prescription frames, and after another three years of research the firm applied the technology to sunglass styles. Advance demand was unprecedented: in the United Kingdom it was reported in August 1981 that the range had already sold out until mid-1982. Typical costs ranged from £27 for a ski goggle to £1100 for a solid 14-carat-gold pair of sunglasses with interchangeable lenses.

From 1981 to 1985 the optical range was developed by Udo Proksch (see Viennaline/ Serge Kirchhofer, p. 87) and the frames were promoted by the Austrian racing driver and airline proprietor Niki Lauda. Lauda was an interesting choice of celebrity ambassador for a facial accessory, since although he represented everything of the daring and adventure the brand wanted to encapsulate, he had also been badly disfigured in an accident in 1976, suffering permanent scarring to his eyelids and the almost total loss of his right ear. The brand got an international boost thanks to Yoko Ono's appearance at a press conference in 1984 in the unconventional Porsche 5620 frame. This model had facial padding around the rims and could accommodate interchangeable sides; the original black models (with prominent white branding) were later joined by gold- and rhodium-plated options. A rimless Porsche model was available from 1986, following on from the supra model 5627.

An article in *Optometry Today* of February 1990, headlined 'Do Cars Sell Sunglasses?', rubbished the supposed 'engineering' standards of Carrera Porsche. The authoritative British commentator on sunglasses Jack Davey quoted the advertising copy 'You may not need an excuse to purchase a pair of sunglasses from the Porsche Design Studios. They are designed by engineers', but in a harsh riposte he suggested that these engineers must have worked on the notorious East German Trabant car.

June 1995 saw the introduction of the Carrera Porsche FO.9 sunglasses, which folded flat (hence the letter F in the name) in two seconds to a height of 0.9 millimetres (less than $1/16$ in.), with the frame separating from the lenses, and available in metallic blue or grey and with round or square rims. The design was said to be the brainchild of Ferdinand Porsche himself. But in 1996 the Carrera-Optyl Group was bought by the Italian Safilo Group, and the Carrera brands were relaunched with fashion direction by John Galliano and the design input of Enzo Sopracolle. Aware that its target customers were buying vintage Carrera frames over the Internet, Safilo launched a Carrera Vintage range, reissuing some of the original designs from the 1980s. New to the Carrera line was the introduction of Flexolite memory metal, which, among other things, represented the first time that Safilo had offered women's ophthalmic frames under the Carrera brand.

Porsche Design sunglasses were relaunched in 1997 by Bausch & Lomb (see Ray-Ban, p. 67), which targeted them at men aged over thirty who like fast cars. The four original designs, Boxster, Proton, T1 and Flow, were sold through car dealers. The company suggested that the adjustable

Porsche Design receiving a prize at Britain's Optrafair in 2009.

Porsche Design P8155 (2010) in titanium, made in Japan. The fenestrated side requires two joints at each rim.

Carrera Porsche Design folding model 5622, 1980s.

Porsche Design's P8801 reading spectacles of 2010 demonstrate that even functional eyewear for the over-forties can be stylish.

The German firm Rodenstock, which bought the licence for Porsche Design in 2001, pioneered the use of celebrities for brand promotion. This advertisement for Rodenstock's own brand from 1960 features Sophia Loren promoting its sunglasses.

The Carrera Porsche Design 5658 of 1988 (far right), with fully adjustable bridge width and leather nose pad (opposite).

Another Rodenstock advertisement from 1960 features German racing driver Wolfgang Graf Berghe von Trips wearing Telecolor lenses for motoring in hazy weather.

bridge achieved 'the nearest thing to a custom fit'. Promoted as 'precision engineering for eyes', the later Tach style featured a screw that enabled the frame shape to be altered. Porsche Design eyewear was available with prescription lenses after 1998.

In 2001 the licence for the Porsche Design brand was acquired by Rodenstock. Founded in 1877, this German company had been rebuilt after the Second World War under Dr Rolf Rodenstock, enjoying success with such plastic frames as the Senator, Rodina and Rocco. It exported in bulk to the United States and Japan, despite those countries' own frame industries and high import tariffs. In the mid-1950s Rodenstock claimed that it was 'probably the first European frame manufacturer to commence advertising in the large illustrated and glossy magazines', and in the 1960s its new styled range of frames included the bestselling Exclusiv and Young Look. In the 1990s Rodenstock sold off its optical machinery and instrument interests, looking to 'think spectacles' in the twenty-first century, having already held the licence for Cerutti for a number of years. It launched a Reebok Eyewear range in 2001 just as it

signed the deal with Ferdinand Alexander Porsche, who described the new partnership (to be managed by Rodenstock's NiGura subsidiary in Düsseldorf) as 'a high concordance of brand understanding and design aspiration'. The plan was to sell 100,000 frames a year.

In 2003 the model P1001 won the Award of Excellence of the United States' Optical Laboratories Association for best sunglasses. Also known as 'the Original', because it was a reinterpretation of the first Porsche Design model of 1978, the P1001 had sides with a 3D design and integrated spring hinges. The P3006, launched in 2003, had clip-in polycarbonate lenses slotted into a metal upper rim and a lower rim made of nylon thread; in effect, it was a supra. In 2007 Porsche Design launched Reading Tools, a masculine half-eye supplied with an ergonomic self-opening hard steel case. This is perhaps part of the brand's main interest to historians – as a fashion eyewear brand appealing to men.

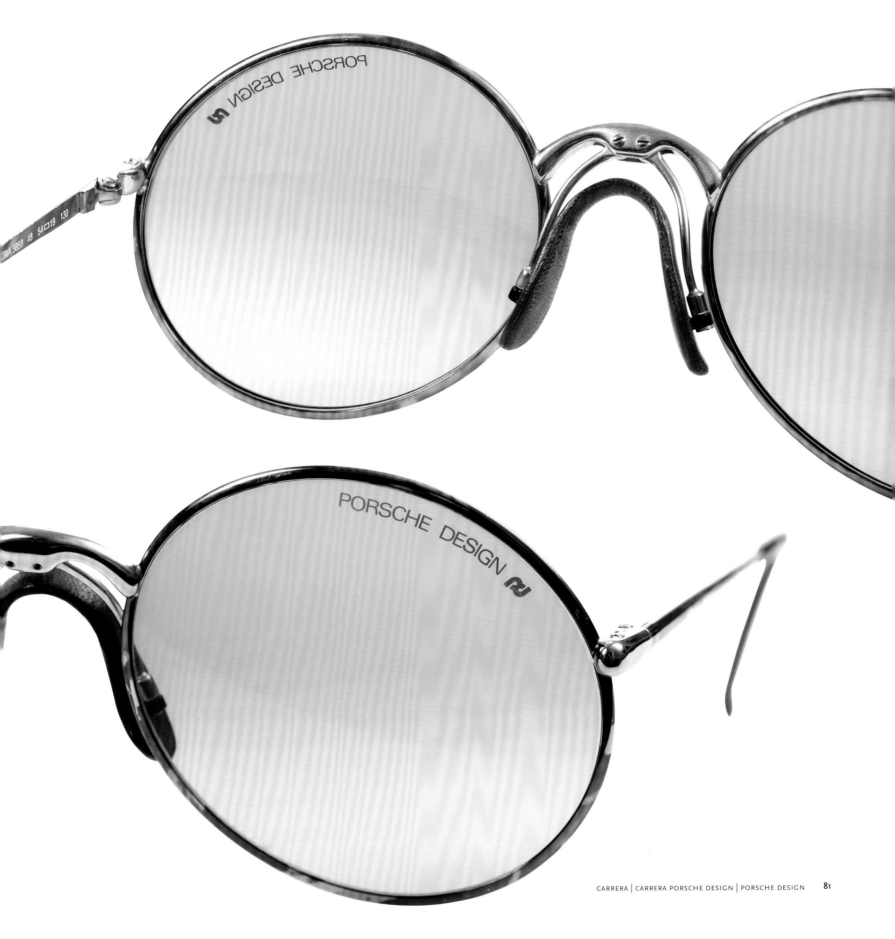

Michael Birch

Known principally for his revolutionary Perspex supra frames from the 1950s to the early 1970s, Michael H. Birch (1926–2008) couldn't resist a business opportunity, and his commercial restlessness ultimately was his undoing. He then gave up the manufacturing business to become an artist, and continued with a career no less extraordinary.

Raised in Egypt of Anglo-French parents, Birch, a trained airman, arrived in England in 1945 as an artist and dancer. He soon had a late-night cabaret act and boasted of selling a sculpture to Henry Moore; at other times he worked in an ice-cream factory and on a building site. He first designed spectacles for the pioneering British frame designer Stanley Unger in Tunbridge Wells, Kent (where he met his future business partner, Brian Green), but was sacked in 1954; with capital of £15, he set up his own business based in his sitting room. The early Birch frames were worked in Perspex from ICI, until Birch hired a chemist and found out how to make his own. He also experimented with fibreglass (and made boats for a few years), and branched out into vacuum-forming after noticing the small plastic trays in which his neighbour

imported fruit. This butterfly approach to business ventures underlines the fact that Birch was essentially a 'small guy', but he is remembered as one who chose to work with 'big' people, such as the moulding expert John Harold.

Birch co-founded the Birch and Green frame-making company in the mid-1950s, eventually settling the business in a former biscuit factory in Tunbridge Wells, and by 1958 he employed thirty people. He was quoted in October 1964 in a supplement of the journal *Optician*: 'My method ... was to start with a datum line on a blank piece of paper and sketch out the basis of an idea. This was then modified over and over again on the same piece of paper, by erasing and redefining lines until I had gone as far as I thought possible in graphic form.' He was determined to maintain quality; it is claimed he once angrily jumped up and down on some frames that emerged too thin from the moulding process.

The Mirage supra frame of the mid-1950s was Birch's first success; advertisements showed it wrapped round the winged mascot of a Rolls Royce. At one point two hundred a day were being produced (three times that number when other supra styles

BIRCH'S CANDI-DOLL

DESIGNED BY MICHAEL BIRCH MSIA

☐ IN ACRILITE · NON-FLAMMABLE · UNBREAKABLE
☐ SIX GORGEOUS ONYX COLOURS
☐ REGULATION 12 · DEEPER EYESHAPE
☐ 18,20,22 DBL · PAD BRIDGE
☐ ACRILITE MOTIF OR GOLD ALUM SIDES
☐ EVERY FRAME GUARANTEED TROUBLE-FREE

Trade promotion for the Candi-Doll, late 1960s.

Michael Birch in 1964 with a cigarette in one hand and a frame in the other, perhaps symbolizing the risky balancing act his multifarious business ventures entailed.

OPPOSITE
New China Doll supra design, 1967.

1

2

3

4

5

6

1
'The best in the world': the Birch catalogue from 1964 is not modest in its claims.

2
Concorde Sunglasses, a range issued in 1978, some years after Michael Birch's departure.

3
Unglazed Mischief supra frame, c. 1958–64. Its inner right side (not visible on this picture) bears the number of the patent that Neville Chappell took out on the supra style in 1941.

4
Swi-Sue, with sinuous sides, 1960s.

5
Masculine Mirage, c. 1964.

6
Pollyanna, c. 1964.

are included); the Rolls-Royce of the advertisement might as well have belonged to the holder of the supra patent, Neville Chappell, since Birch had to pay him five shillings for each Mirage sold. Birch bought out his partner and renamed the company Michael H. Birch Designs. He then took over his largest wholesale distributor, Stigmat, against the wishes of that firm's then owner, Reg Reid, forming the Michael Birch Group. He also built a new factory from scratch, and took over the premises next door.

Birch developed an interest in acetate sheet in about 1961, thus becoming involved with Max Wiseman, founder of the Algha Works (p. 55), who made the reinforcement wires for him. Wiseman also made all Birch's aluminium sides, meeting such a large demand that for a while the Wiseman factory in Mauchline, Scotland, produced little else. Birch's aim was for his own factory to be the most modern in the world, so he bought all the most advanced and expensive German machines. Chemical company British Celanese filmed the launch of its Rocel acetate material at the Birch factory, because the plant looked so modern and clean. In 1966 Birchware was founded to supply sunglasses and protective eyewear. Originally this was the name of the tableware range John Harold made for Birch, but it came to be applied to the whole moulding department. Polaroid (p. 63) was a major customer.

By 1970 Birch was recognized as the most automated frame factory in Europe, producing 2000 frames a day, of which 400 (one-fifth of the entire production) were the Candi-Doll, a plastic frame with a very pointed upper rim bearing a contrasting coloured trim. The company sold mainly in Britain but did maintain an American sales office for a short while. At one point Birch had no fewer than five factories. The company also took over factories for electronic components and musical drums. In 1970, however, Birch unexpectedly took a back seat and the company was bought by merchant bankers J. Henry Schroder Wagg, and there were serious arguments over the business accounts. The basic ophthalmic business was judged to be sound, but unwise acquisitions in other areas had caused losses that even the auditors had missed.

In 1972 Birch resigned from the boards of all the subsidiaries, and from then on worked with them in an advisory capacity only. In time-honoured fashion, it was reported that he wished 'to devote more time to his other activities', and in this instance that was possibly true. In his mid-forties Birch became a highly successful professional carver of Japanese *netsuke* (miniature carvings) and a maker of hand-crafted books.

In the 1950s and 1960s, at a time of German and Austrian dominance in the sector, Michael Birch flew the British flag for fashion-orientated eyewear. The Birch catalogue from 1978 (far left) shows a designer continuing the tradition of using dummy heads to check the appearance of frames.

This women's supra model is very similar to that chosen by the novelist Agatha Christie, but she wore less angled lenses. The appeal of Birch frames to the older generation should not obscure the impact his designs made at a time of NHS frame dominance, when few private frames succeeded commercially in Britain.

Mirage, *c.* 1970.

Fantasy Damask, 1970s.

Viennaline | Serge Kirchhofer

Often regarded as the first widely distributed fashion eyewear label, Viennaline enjoyed a remarkable longevity. Although it eventually settled down as a mid-price range, after its launch in 1958 it was synonymous with European eyewear fashion. As such it was the first range to raise the hackles of those opticians who questioned whether spectacles should be marketed in this way. Yet when the Austrian Wilhelm (Willie) Anger (born 1926) launched his first fashion ophthalmic frames in 1951, his range was just one of several already available, including the German-made Rodina by Rodenstock, Bonira by Marwitz and Gigant by Metzler, the French Amor range and the British Michael Birch (p. 83).

Founded in 1948 to make protective goggles for welders, Anger OHG began manufacturing spectacle frames in cellulose nitrate and metal in 1951. Anger, who at the time of writing was still introducing new innovations to the eyewear market after more than sixty years, was a forceful figure from the start. If he saw something he liked, or had an idea for a design, it had to be so. It is said he once instructed that a dead tree near the factory be painted blue rather than chopped down.

Zart (*c.* 1963) featured a faux wooden hood to the upper rim.

Viennaline — DIE LINIE MODISCHEN WIENER GESCHMACKS

In the 1950s Viennaline was promoted as a tasteful fashion line from Vienna, a city of high culture, music and dance.

Anger was determined to introduce more sophistication to his products, and the Doublé frame of 1953 and the subsequent range of gold frames mark the beginning of that quest. The big hit of 1955 was Papagena, and other bestsellers included the Gigi and Alt-Wien (Old Vienna) models. In 1954 Anger met Udo Proksch, the winner of a student frame-design competition. The creative genius of the German-born Proksch (1934–2001) has been eclipsed in the public record by his descent into criminality.

OPPOSITE
Victoria 439, pictured in the first issue of the *Anger-Brillen-Kurier* 'lifestyle' magazine (January 1958) published by Viennaline founder Willie Anger.

Udo Proksch, designer of the Viennaline and Serge Kirchhofer lines, had a colourful personal life. He was the first husband of actress Daphne Wagner, and his friends included racing driver James Hunt, King Hussein of Jordan and Leonid Brezhnev, head of the Soviet Communist Party. In 1991 Proksch was jailed for his part in an insurance fraud that resulted in the death of six people.

Alfred Kleissner, a craftsman who in the 1960s worked on the Viennaline and Serge Kirchhofer lines.

Serge Kirchhofer logo and butterfly motif.

Pages of a Viennaline catalogue from 1966.

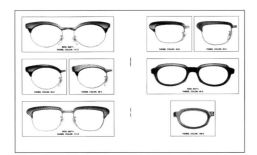

Proksch began innocently enough, after a spell as a pig farmer and a radio evangelist, designing ski masks for Carrera. The inevitable interest in his political activities, arms smuggling and murder of six people aboard the ship *Lucona* in 1977 as part of an insurance fraud, followed by his years of evading justice under the protection of the Viennese political elite, risk obscuring the fact that he was one of the most influential figures in the history of designer eyewear.

With Proksch's design input Anger launched Viennaline in 1958 as a fully branded range. Proksch later claimed the name as his idea. It was undeniably an inspired choice, conjuring up the grandeur of the Habsburg capital and the excitement of the Cold War centre of intrigue as conveyed so memorably in the film *The Third Man* (1949); most importantly, the word was easily understood in many languages.

By 1960 Anger had developed the Serge Kirchhofer (SK) luxury line. Proksch chose the first name Serge as a reflection of his Communist political leanings, after the Trotskyist writer Victor Serge; as regards the name Kirchhofer, one story has it that this was the surname of a girlfriend of Proksch, another that he thought of the name (which translates as 'churchyard') while standing in a graveyard. (Proksch's love of cemeteries prompted him in 1970 to promote a madcap scheme for

vertical burials, so that those whose lives had been far from upright could at least 'go straight' in death.)

It had been planned that Proksch would work with Anger's sister, Anneliese (who later became a fierce competitior to her brother after she married Arnold Schmied, founder of Silhouette; p. 103), but they did not succeed together. Proksch therefore worked on a freelance basis, receiving commission on sales – a lucrative arrangement for him, considering that one of his styles for Viennaline, the Gigi, is believed to have sold 15 million pieces. The factory was at Traun, near Linz, but Proksch was provided with his own studio in the centre of Vienna, in which two people were employed to make samples. Proksch also supervised all photography and the design of sales display material: hand-held mirrors for optical practices (in 1962), for example, and a scarf, intended for window display, but which all the opticians took home for their wives.

At around this time the brand became available in Britain; by 1967 this market was of sufficient size that subsidiary British company Viennaline Ltd was established under Erwin Stern, who knew the British taste, having previously worked in the United Kingdom in the 1930s. Proksch's brother, Rüdiger, developed the SK brand through advertising, and Walter Pichler designed the SK logo and corporate image, including the distinctive butterfly that was central to SK window displays. In the early 1970s, each exclusive new SK range 'designed by this master designer in Vienna' was presented on the Viennaline stand at trade shows.

Anger's greatest contribution to the sector was perhaps his championing of injection-moulded sunglasses. The apogee of this movement was in 1967, when the firm introduced its new Optyl epoxy-resin plastic (which had been under development since 1963) on a trial basis, anonymously and with some teething problems. Optyl was meant to be cheap and easy to mass-produce, but that aim was not fulfilled. Nevertheless, following Optyl's official introduction a few years later, Viennaline frames were 20–30 per cent lighter and also more stable, owing to the absence of any plasticizer in the material. The first Optyl frames were the Club 21 series, which had a remarkably hard surface that retained polish well and sides so rigid they did not require metal reinforcement.

Optyl was launched in 1968 to great fanfare at a conference in Vienna, with demonstrations of the material properties; lead scientist Dr G. Hampel delighted in tying up a heated frame in knots to show how it relaxed back into its original shape on cooling. Given the unusual prominence accorded to a technical designer, it is bizarre that in 2010 the Italian Safilo Group launched a marketing campaign to promote Optyl, which it now controlled, pretending that the material had been discovered in 1970 by (fictitious) scientist Fridebald Schulz. The final form of Optyl was in fact not perfected until 1971. Optyl was such a success that its name was also given to a separate company within Anger's group.

Udo Proksch, meanwhile, designed his famous Goldfinger range of jewellery and objects, including an ornamental silver shoe that looked like an unshod foot, and

Viennaline Marc (date unknown) with its original box.

The Serge Kirchhofer archive in Vienna retains frames alongside their original drawings and designer's notes (far left). Proksch designed on whatever lay to hand, as with this colourful signed drawing on a piece of paper that is missing its corner.

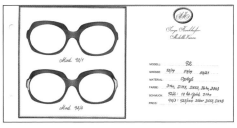

A product catalogue entry for Serge Kirchhofer model 92 in Optyl, c. 1968–72.

A Viennaline promotional shot, 1960s.

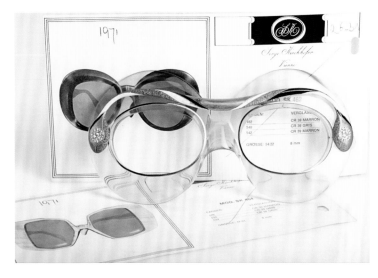

A poster from 1972 showing the Serge Kirchhofer frame no. 500, part of the SK Legion Mystique promotion featuring model Elisabeth Fallenberg.

A prototype of an SK women's spectacle front from the early 1970s (above, right), and catalogue illustrations from the same era.

A Serge Kirchhofer frame from 1970.

Serge Kirchhofer 462, 1971.

Serge Kirchhofer model 480, early 1970s.

in 1972 shocked the Viennese establishment by buying the former royal bakery and purveyor of the finest cakes, Demel, on the Kohlmarkt. This soon became the meeting place for the notorious Club 45, an association of politicians from the ruling Austrian Socialist party, the SPÖ, and for Syrian arms dealers with links to the Palestinian Liberation Organization. One of the most bizarre schemes Proksch hatched through Club 45 was a project to establish an Austrian military museum, to which some serious artillery was donated, only to be 'stolen'; much of this weaponry apparently ended up in the Middle East.

In 1972 Proksch ran Serge Kirchhofer on his own (without Anger) for a short while via his production company, Optico, but soon afterwards he sold the SK name to Baron R.R. Drasche-Wartinberg, who handed over the range's distribution to Argus Optik. Proksch remained as chief designer for the range and stamped his own designs 'UDO'. He designed on whatever lay to hand: some sketches in his archive have phone numbers noted on them; one design is on a Demel napkin, another on a beer mat.

In 1977, as we now know, Proksch carried out a major insurance fraud, loading what was labelled as uranium mining equipment (in reality scrap machinery) and insured for 31 million Swiss francs on to a freighter, and detonating the lot in the middle of the Indian Ocean. Six people died, but six others survived to make testimony. Proksch, however, was protected by the establishment, and it proved impossible to pin anything on him until a change of government, the first for a generation, in 1983. Demel was raided and incriminating documents were found, although it took a further five years to build a proper case.

In the meantime there had been an abortive attempt to launch the Serge Kirchhofer range in Britain in 1980. In this period Proksch also designed for Alfred Dunhill (licensed to Optyl in 1982) and Christian Dior (p. 109). He last designed professionally in 1987. Following the publication in 1988 of the book *Der Fall Lucona* by Hans Pretterebner, about the scandal, Proksch fled to the Philippines, where he attempted to disguise his identity with plastic surgery to his face. Rashly passing through London's Heathrow airport in 1990, he was spotted and was returned to Vienna. Paradoxically, the years of delay had actually increased the chances of securing a conviction, because the wreck of the *Lucona* had recently been located by forensic investigators, who were determined to bring Proksch to justice. He was jailed in 1991 and died ten years later. Proksch's colourful life has been the subject of a stage musical, *Udo 77* (2004), and a major documentary by Austrian director Robert Dornhelm, *Out of Control* (2010) – although not much was made of his career in eyewear design.

In 1978 Anger sold all his shares in the Optyl company to the Hamburg publishing firm Heinrich Bauer Verlag, but remained as managing director. In the 1980s there were five designers for the Optyl eyewear ranges, resident in Germany, Sweden, Italy, France and Spain. This was a period of remarkable productivity and innovation. In 1982 it was reported that half of Optyl's production was of new styles, and the company was making some ten million frames a year at factories in Vienna and Traun, while components might also be produced at plants in Yugoslavia, Germany and Canada. Despite this vast manufacturing empire, demand for the company's newest brand, Carrera Porsche Design (p. 77) was reported to be outstripping capacity. In 1996 the Carrera-Optyl Group was bought by the Italian Safilo Group.

A men's frame from the 1980s, bearing the Serge Kirchhofer signature on the inner side.

Viennaline 1040 (*c.* 1990), with V-shaped matt-finish soldered bridge.

Viennaline 1093, *c.* 1990.

Vuarnet

Vuarnet, the French sunglasses brand that has been associated with skiers since it was set up in 1960, once described itself as 'the brand that goes downhill – fast'. To some extent, after its 1980s heyday, that is what happened to it, until in 2010 it started hauling itself back up the mountain.

In 1951 Joseph Hatchiguian was taken on as an apprentice in the Paris optical practice of Roger Pouilloux, which had been founded nine years earlier. Hatchiguian went on to develop the Skilynx lens to combat glare at high altitude, and this was introduced to the market by Sporoptic Pouilloux in 1957. The lens became a favourite of the renowned French skier Jean Vuarnet (born 1933), who, in common with many in the sport, appreciated it for the clarity of vision it afforded, whatever the weather. He felt that when he was crossing snowy bumps at speed the lens helped him to judge the relief of the terrain, especially when the light was poor. Whether it was the lenses or his talent for downhill racing that propelled him to greatness, the fact remains that Vuarnet was wearing Pouilloux lenses when he won a gold medal in the men's downhill at the 1960 Winter Olympics in Squaw Valley, California. Seizing the

moment, Pouilloux and Vuarnet launched a range of sunglasses with lenses designed by Hatchiguian (who would eventually rise to become president of the Vuarnet brand).

Aimed at the adventurous, Vuarnet sunglasses prompted American tourists to enter alpine shops and demand the glasses called 'Warnay'. An inability to pronounce the name correctly rarely prevented a sale, however, and a period of rapid growth began, bolstered by significant brand exposure at the 1984 Summer Olympics in Los Angeles. In January 1987 *Optometry Today* reported that Vuarnet were 'the world's most prestigious sun and sports glasses' and the bestselling in the United States, where the firm paid women's tennis champion Martina Navratilova $4 million in sponsorship fees.

The range at that time was manufactured almost exclusively from plastic materials; many of the frames were of flexible nylon and therefore practically unbreakable if a wearer took a fall on the snow or a tennis ball in the face. But like its younger rival, Revo, Vuarnet sold itself primarily on the strength of its lenses rather than that of its frames. Both brands were noted for mirrored lenses offered in a range

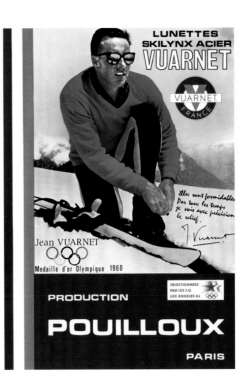

This poster produced in advance of the 1984 Summer Olympics, held in Los Angeles, makes bold and colourful use of retro imagery to promote the Vuarnet brand. Already well established in Europe, Vuarnet soon took America by storm.

OPPOSITE
The French skier Jean Vuarnet in goggles with Skilynx lenses, later used in Vuarnet sunglasses, on his way to victory in the downhill race at the 1960 Winter Olympics.

of colours. Vuarnet had four main lines: the semi-mirrored amber Skilynx; the brown PX2000, a lighter lens for motorists or for use in summer conditions; the dark brown PX5000 for high-level mountaineering; and the amber Nautilux, with reflective bands, marketed to sailing enthusiasts.

Despite having wrapped up its market, Vuarnet was aware of the need to make its frames more interesting. At Britain's Optrafair in 1991 the company offered styles that were visibly reminiscent of the 1960s. Vuarnet was consciously aiming to tap into the mainstream optical fashion market, offering stylish frames in hand-finished acetate to sit alongside its nylon sport range; unlike the sport range, the acetate frames were not guaranteed against accidental damage. When the PX3000 lens was launched in 1992, it was capable of taking an ophthalmic prescription. The Vuarnet brand also diversified into leisure-wear, ski clothing, footwear (in association with Royer), perfume, high-performance watches, writing implements, sports luggage, travel insurance for skiers, and even a four-wheel-drive vehicle launched in collaboration with Suzuki.

Jean Vuarnet retired in 1998 and handed over the business to his sons, Alain and Pierre, both of them sportsmen as much as they were entrepreneurs. Soon Vuarnet began licensing products as diverse as helmets and tanning lotions, and teamed up with a pharmaceutical laboratory to offer nutritional supplements that were promoted as slowing down the ageing effects of exposure to the sun. Not forgetting its origins as an eyewear brand, Vuarnet offered the Mountaineer and Glaciers ranges with

distinctive leather side shields suitable for climbers. The Glaciers models, such as the 031 in injection-moulded nylon, were intended to replace the classic styles worn by mountain guides and other workers at high altitude.

By 2009 Vuarnet was a shadow of its former self, its turnover having fallen from the equivalent of 28 million in 1990 to just 10 million. Alain Mikli International (p. 135) bought 75 per cent of Sporoptic Pouilloux in 2010, and, as the new designer for the range, Mikli presented his first Vuarnet collection later that year, ahead of its commercial launch in 2011. With such a big name behind the brand, the forecast was bright for Vuarnet once again as it reached its fiftieth anniversary.

Model 056, a streamlined egg shape (above and left), date unknown. Vuarnet sunglasses have traditionally been sold at ski resorts rather than through opticians. The original owner of this pair bought them at a sunglasses shop in the French ski resort of Isola 2000.

Model 006, date unknown.

Neostyle

When styled spectacles were still new, along came Neostyle. Walter A. Nufer (1934–2001) founded Neostyle Nufer Optik in 1961 in the German town of Gerlingen, a manufacturing town on the outskirts of Stuttgart known for its watchmaking and jewellery industries. Nufer's story is similar to that of the Schmieds in Linz (see Silhouette, p. 103) or of Tony Gross in London (see Cutler and Gross, p. 113). Put simply, Nufer wanted to design spectacle frames that might be considered fashion accessories, not just functional vision aids, and his guiding mantra was the phrase 'personality design'.

The brand was introduced to the United States in 1970 and shortly afterwards received a significant boost when it was worn by Elvis Presley (see p. 101), whose endorsement ensured international exposure. Neostyle UK was founded by Derek Roberts in Manchester in 1974, making it one of the first German brands to challenge the domestic market in Britain. In the mid-1970s the company's marketing slogan was 'Precise in production. Foremost in fashion', and it was this combination of stylish looks and high quality of manufacture that gave the brand an early boost outside Germany.

Walter A. Nufer, founder of the firm.

Society 105, 1974.

Society 155, 1978.

Sunart 775, c. 1974–75.

OPPOSITE
A Neostyle promotional image from the 1970s.

97

Mondial, *c.* 1980.

Office 6, 1987.

Rotary 20, 1974.

Dynasty 362, 1995.

In the mid-1970s Neostyle designed the Sunart collection, introduced in English-speaking countries in about 1980 under the slogan 'Wherever there is sun and fashion'. The Society range, which included the popular models 150 for men and 155 for women, with their fenestrated two-part rims, was launched in 1978. At that time the parent company employed 200 people at its base factory in Gerlingen, plus another 250 in manufacturing plants in the Black Forest and France, and was exporting to at least ninety countries.

The house brand, Neostyle Couture Eyewear, was under the direction of chief designer Konstantin Livas, the man behind the famous Nautic frame, who produced one model from 18-carat gold studded with diamonds. The company also liaised with Italian couturier Renato Balestra, who put his name to two women's collections, Gregoriana and Sistina. Balestra and Nufer went on to sponsor their own fashion shows in major cities. In 1982 Balestra designed the Firenze ophthalmic range, the Via Veneto range (named after the famous Roman shopping street) and the Gran Cala range in precious metals. Some of these were in 18-carat gold, as were frames in the Dynasty range shown at Germany's Optica trade fair in 1986 – the name suggesting the lavish lifestyles seen in the popular American soap opera starring Linda Evans and Joan Collins. (Another screen icon, Elizabeth Taylor, who so memorably played a member of the Greek Ptolemaic dynasty when she took on the role of Cleopatra in the 1960s, was known

Academic 45 with beach lenses, 1981.

Jet 46 with asymmetric bridge, *c*. 1992. This model is a sort of nylon supra, but the cord is at the side rather than underneath. The Jet range has been worn by Kim Basinger, Demi Moore and Oprah Winfrey (and the men's range by Burt Reynolds and the techno musician Richard Melville Hall, better known by his stage name, Moby).

Boutique 307, 1974.

College 39 (1980) on its original card.

Academic 50, 1981.

Colosseo RB 410, designed by Renato Balestra in the 1980s. The Italian couturier originally studied civil engineering. His collaboration with Neostyle sealed his entry into eyewear.

to wear this range.) Neostyle at this time was emphasizing the feminine ranges; Cambridge Optical Group, which had taken over distribution in Britain, made news when it promoted the brand at Britain's Optrafair in 1986 with an all-female sales force.

In the early 1990s Neostyle had most success in mainland Europe, and its frames took on consciously European themes: foremost was the collection of 'personality' frames, such as the Mozart anniversary frame, launched in 1991, and the sporty Superstar 1 and the Academic models that aimed to promote the 'college' look typified by Harold Lloyd (see p. 53), albeit without a hint of retro shape or style. In 1996 Neostyle introduced the Forum collection, featuring a new wire-bending technique, and in 1997 the company announced its plans to focus on 'trend' frames, launching the Holiday sunglasses collection. New materials, including a cobalt alloy, were tried around 1998 in the College range, and rimless styles came to the fore, meaning that Neostyle enjoyed renown for both extravagant and minimalist designs.

Elvis Presley

(1935–1977) American popular singer

Personalized spectacles made for Elvis Presley by Hans Fiebig of Optique Boutique in Los Angeles, and the original mould for Presley's TCB ('Taking Care of Business') flash produced by San Francisco jeweller Ludwig Schwarte in 1969.

Since his death Elvis Presley has been portrayed by numerous impersonators in black wigs, white jumpsuits, medallions and sunglasses. This stereotypical image of popular music's first mega-brand reflects only the later look of the 'king of rock 'n' roll'. In the 1950s he wore black leathers and futuristic wraparound aviator-style frames by Renauld, with front and side lenses suspended from a bar.

Presley was constantly reinventing himself. In his young days he was his own stylist, experimenting with a 'ghetto fabulous' look sourced from such shops as Lansky Bros in Memphis, Tennessee, where he had moved as a teenager from his birthplace in Tupelo, Mississippi. When he came out of the army, in 1960, fans and critics alike hailed the voice behind 'It's Now or Never' as the 'new Elvis'. This evolution was carefully managed, and historians have tracked his

alternating tendency towards wearing black or white. Presley told his wife, Priscilla, that he preferred solid colours to printed designs and that he hated brown and dark green, which he associated with the army.

Presley's confidence grew in the late 1960s, and he eventually transmuted into an über-personality with hair dyed jet-black to highlight his blue eyes. In 1969, backed by a thirty-piece orchestra, he took to the stage of the International Hotel (later renamed the Hilton) in Las Vegas, Nevada, for his first live appearances in more than eight years, signing a five-year agreement at $100,000 a week, and went on to perform a total of 837 shows. In the officially filmed concerts Presley did not wear sunglasses, but he appears with them frequently in the films documenting these years, such as *Elvis on Tour* (1972). He also wore sunglasses when being presented with a Federal

Agent's badge from President Richard Nixon in 1970. Presley was obsessed with control mechanisms – badges and guns. Perhaps the dark glasses were part of that desire to exude authority.

During his celebrated Madison Square Garden performances in 1972, Presley wore the Nautic model by Neostyle. He wore the largest size (66) and the lens tint was light, so as not to hide his eyes, on which so much of his appeal relied. It was available in gold and silver, and genuine examples now sell online for between £500 and £800.

In the mid-1970s Presley went through a phase of liking all things to do with Grand Prix motor racing. He personalized his sunglasses, which were in gold or chrome, with the letters TCB ('Taking Care of Business') picked out in white gold on the sides, and his own initials, EP, in the fenestration between the bridge and the browbar. Dennis Roberts and Hans

Fiebig of Optique Boutique in Los Angeles supplied in excess of 400 pairs to Presley over his lifetime, charging around $500 a pair. Fiebig recalled their meeting in a letter to this book's author:

One day, around 1969, I saw Elvis cruising Sunset Strip, right in front of our store. I gave him my business card and he thanked me. A few days later, he came in to our store with his entire entourage. He noticed that we had quite a selection of frames. He stated to me exactly what he was looking for. He had with him a very inexpensive 'drug store'-type frame. It was an aviator shape, had a metallic look and had holes on the side of the temples. He really liked the way these looked on him. Elvis was wearing a necklace with a very large lightning bolt and 'TCB' on it. He was wondering if I could add this to the side of the temples. And while

I was at it, could I put his initials on the bridge? I realized at that time that you couldn't 'sell' Elvis anything – he had very specific ideas about what he liked and what he wanted – either you could do it or you couldn't. Of course I told him we could and I figured I would work out the details later.

In death, of course, there was nothing Presley could do to control the manner in which his 'brand' continued. Genuine souvenirs of the man quickly achieved astronomical prices. The book *Dead Elvis: A Chronical of a Cultural Obsession* (1991) by American music critic Greil Marcus examined the afterlife of Presley's image. In Britain 'exact replica' sunglasses were available in silver- and gold-coloured rims for about £9 from the Elvisly Yours business, established in 1979 by Sid Shaw.

Silhouette

O nce renowned for its futuristic large plastic frames, Silhouette took a remarkable strategic decision in the late 1990s to concentrate its design efforts on rimless spectacles and then, in 2009, to confine its output to them, thereby attempting to redefine the nature of the cult as 'seeing without boundaries'. Its products are so lightweight that it has succeeded in dominating the market for spectacles worn in space (some 90 per cent of astronauts wear spectacles, such are the stresses on the eye of working in space).

1

Silhouette was founded in Linz, Austria, in 1964 by the optical toolmaker Arnold Schmied and his wife, Anneliese (both born 1925). As a later slogan put it, they wanted clients to 'enjoy wearing glasses'. They began this endeavour with a female designer, Dora Demmel (born 1938), and five employees, selling to four countries, but two years later they were supplying most of Western Europe. In different circumstances the designer's name might have become the brand's name. Demmel was

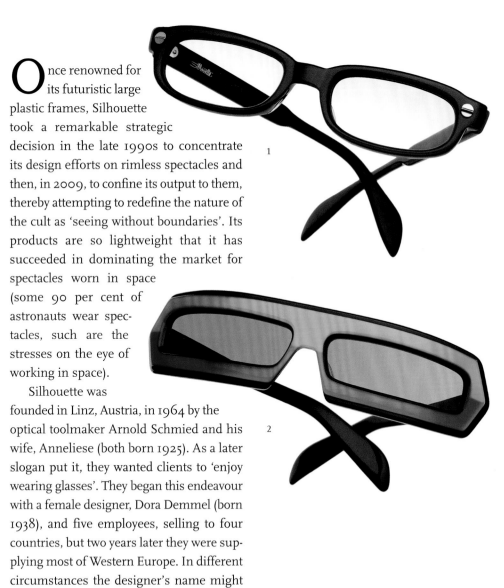

2

1
The first Silhouette frame, model no. 1, 1964.

2
Model 606 from the first sunglasses range, 1967.

3
Arnold Schmied founded Silhouette with his wife, Anneliese, in 1964. In 1987 he marvelled: 'Two rims, two side pieces, a few square millimetres of material – how can these limited elements repeatedly form the basis of new designs? And yet artists actually manage to produce new creations.'

4
Klaus and Arnold Schmied Jr, sons of the founders and the current co-directors of Silhouette. In 2007 Arnold Schmied Jr claimed that Silhouette was no longer in the 'fashion' business but in facial 'cosmetics'.

5
Dora Demmel, Silhouette's first designer.

3

4

5

OPPOSITE
A promotion for Futura sunglasses, 1974.

The first issue of Silhouette's *Couture* magazine, from 1972, featured a cover by French fashion illustrator René Gruau.

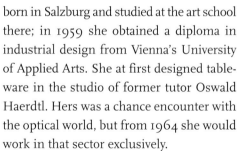

Model 417, nicknamed 'the Temptress', 1972.

Futura 570, 1974.

Model 607, launched in 1969.

born in Salzburg and studied at the art school there; in 1959 she obtained a diploma in industrial design from Vienna's University of Applied Arts. She at first designed tableware in the studio of former tutor Oswald Haerdtl. Hers was a chance encounter with the optical world, but from 1964 she would work in that sector exclusively.

Demmel's sunglass designs were originally intended simply for shop-window displays, but became products in their own right; by 1987 she had designed nearly 10,000 frames, and some 1500 of them had come on to the market. She always started a design with rough sketches, which she then followed up with more precise enlarged drawings, and she both supervised and assisted in making the handmade samples from which prototypes were made after facial fitting had been tested.

Demmel introduced coloured pin covers on acetate lugs in 1966, and designed a coloured metal range in 1973. Her most famous product was the oversized Futura range of about 1973–74, which came in lurid orange or green plastic. The ability to supply the Futura range brought prominence to Silhouette's British distributor, the Grafton Optical Company, and the Austrian parent company was apparently widely held to have doubled the price in order to make its product seem better. In this period (*c.* 1969–74) some Silhouette frames were manufactured in the German Black Forest, by Menrad.

What set Silhouette apart was its marketing, notably carried out in the pages of its in-house magazine, *Couture* (produced until 1992). The marketing consisted of articles on all sorts of lifestyle topics, never mentioning the spectacle styles in the text but showing top fashion models wearing Silhouette eyewear in the accompanying illustrations. This was such an alien concept that in the early days the *Couture* editorial team had to take care that the models selected for the photo-shoot would actually wear the spectacles supplied to them, as the models feared it would harm their fashionable image. Carla Bruni and Marcus Schenkenberg, who is regarded as the first male supermodel, are among the Silhouette models who went on to greater things. It is interesting to note that many of the fashion clothing names featured in *Couture* would later license their own eyewear.

In the 1980s the range went by the name Silhouette Fashion Frames. Company name and brand name were synonymous and the value of this was recognized after 1997 when, following a brief hiatus during which the company had been known formally in several territories by the name A. Schmied, the marketing concept of the 'House of Silhouette' was introduced, tied in with the opening of dedicated boutique stores. Freeline, Silhouette's first rimless range, was launched in 1983, but at the time more attention was given to the company's new SPX plastic, which made it possible to make frames with extremely thin rims; before long, these could also be printed with decorative designs.

The key designer of this period was Gerhard Balder, a qualified optician but also a cartoonist who designed jewellery and spectacles, including a bicycle frame for

From the Freeline rimless range, 1983.

Model 7138 from the Cartoon range (1991) repeated designer Gerhard Balder's earlier successful motif of lugs in the form of gripping hands.

Minimal Art model 9706 (1992), the first rimless model made of titanium without hinges.

Titan Minimal Art model 7624 (1999), by Silhouette designer Gerhard Fuchs. The range originally came in two styles and five colours. This design represents late-1990s reduction, stripping eyewear of nearly everything. A titanium alloy allowed the weight to be reduced to 1.8 g (0.063 oz). A Space edition was launched in 2006, and the range is now popular with astronauts.

1
Model 620 combination frame, 1973.

2
Metal Art model 6119, 1990.

3
The ultra-thin frame of Silhouette's SPX plastic, post-1983.

4
Model 551, date unknown.

5
Model 9122 (1994), by Massimo Iosa Ghini, originally a furniture designer, who played with the 'fascination of curves'.

Elton John and a frame featuring enormous hearts and two pianos. President Mobutu of Zaire ordered twenty identical pairs – one for each of his residences. Balder's most famous frame, the Bioframe (named after German chat-show host Alfred Biolek) featured two fists gripping the lugs. Designed in 1984 for the company's twentieth anniversary, the Bioframe was never intended for the market, but eventually 3000 were produced; the frame was relaunched in 1989.

The Titan Minimal Art range of titanium rimless spectacles was designed in 1999 by Gerhard Fuchs (who began work for Silhouette in 1981 aged fifteen as an apprentice toolmaker, but was sent on a design course in 1988 after company founder Arnold Schmied saw some of the young man's drawings). In 2010 it was still the company's bestseller. So phenomenal was the success of this rimless style that in 2009 Silhouette decided to abandon its other lines – or, as the company put it, to abandon the 'cult' of the full frame.

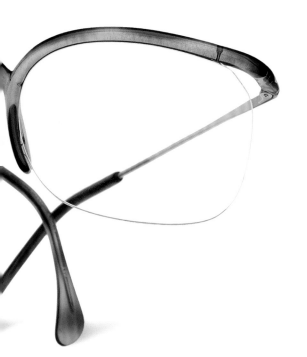

Louis D. Bronson

born Louis Braunstein (1907–1994),
American optometrist

Gas-mask spectacles (1940s) supplied to Canada by American Optical, of the type adapted for resale by Louis D. Bronson (below) in the 1960s and 1970s.

'Dr Bronson digs the young generation. These young people are beautiful he says.' So stated an article entitled 'Era of Groovy Eyeglasses', featured in *Optometric World* in April 1971. Working from Los Angeles, the American Louis D. Bronson was the self-proclaimed optometrist to the 'love generation'. He qualified in 1946, so was unfettered by pre-war attitudes, and was interested in European designer brands, including Dior, Cassini, Pucci, Pierre Cardin and Biki of Italy – a topic of conversation that served him well with his numerous reported women friends during a period when he ran the Queens Bifocal Company in New York. Bronson moved west to California in 1962, and this brought him into contact with very different potential customers.

In July 1968 Bronson was featured in the 'Wailing Nat Freedland' column in the *Free Press of Los Angeles* underground paper, for his practice of fitting modern coloured lenses into antique metal frames. It seems he was already being pestered with requests for 'John Lennon

glasses', particularly from GIs in Vietnam who wanted to identify with peace, love and freedom. Soon he had queues of hippies waiting to buy all the old stock he could source from redundant businesses and long-neglected warehouses; and, for when antiques were not to hand, he developed a method of antiquing new metal frames using electro-plating, basing his technique on that described in the book *Metal Colouring* by David Fishlock, published in England in 1962.

A pioneer of collecting vintage eyewear for commercial resale, Bronson supplied period spectacles for the Hall of Presidents at Walt Disney World in Florida and wrote a book, *Early American Specs: An Exciting Collectible* (1974), in which he claimed he had caused many a Second World War veteran to retrieve from the attic his old 'gas mask frames' (designed to be worn under a gas mask) – that is, if his son, daughter or grandchildren had not got to them first. Regarded by his professional contemporaries as something

of a maverick and remembered by his relatives as both an opportunist and an innovator, Bronson spoke the language of young people without ever really becoming part of their scene. He liked to brag about movie stars coming into his practice, and told the tale of how he had once said to a customer, 'These Peter Fonda types would look great on you', only to elicit the reply, 'I *am* Peter Fonda.'

Christian Dior

The House of Dior is generally acknowledged to have been the first major fashion house to permit its name to be applied to an eyewear brand under licence (in the mid- to late 1960s), which was no small step for its time. The eyewear was remarkably well received, and models from the 1970s and 1980s remain immensely collectible today. The oversized form, with its characteristic fenestrated lugs, has been the subject of much imitation, which is perhaps the ultimate compliment, and the CD logo has become one of the industry's most recognizable.

The fashion house was founded in 1946, and the folk memory of its first collection, the fabled 'New Look' of 1947, perhaps overshadows the fact that the brand had been prepared from the start to explore new areas of business. For example, also in 1947 it established the independent Société des Parfums Christian Dior to market branded fragrances, and the couturier was the first to open a street-level boutique selling accessories. In 1948 Christian Dior (1905–1957) was the first designer to sign a licence agreement in the United States (for stockings), and under the fashion house's president, Jacques Rouët, licensing became

A wraparound ginger opal frame in epoxy resin (Optyl), showing the very short side reinforcements that are characteristic of early frames made from that material, which was launched in 1968. The Christian Dior name first appeared on Optyl frames in the early 1970s.

Model CO1, 1970s.

Model 2026, 1970s. The lens passes over a supplementary rim placed behind it, giving the effect of two apertures.

OPPOSITE
A display mannequin bearing model 2387, c. 1993.

Model 2030, 1970s. Christian Dior was the first couture house to use a logo on luggage and leather goods and the first French house to export these, so branded eyewear was a natural next step. Here the CD logo is visible on the side, largely concealing the short metal reinforcement behind it.

Model 2112, date unknown.

Model 2189, 1980s.

Model 2340 (1980s), featuring 'temples of fragrance' with a compartment for storing a scented sachet.

an overarching strategy, coupled with a preference for local production and locally tailored marketing.

As regards eyewear, Dior at first explored working with the American company Tura, but took the rights away. Wilhelm Anger, the founder of the Austrian Viennaline (p. 87) and Carrera (p. 77) and the man who coined the eyewear slogan 'Dress your face', began negotiations with the House of Dior in 1966; the Christian Dior range of spectacles, manufactured in Austria, became widely available in 1969. It was intended as a range synonymous with luxury, but the idea of a visible brand name was still unfamiliar. The Italian designer Emilio Pucci asked Anger why he had a designer's name on his frame, and how much the designer had been paid to put it there. Anger respectfully corrected Pucci: he had had to pay House of Dior for the right to put it there!

In the early 1970s the Dior range was in the vanguard for Viennaline's new Optyl cast-frame material, being the perfect vehicle for demonstrating that plastic's potential for achieving three-dimensional effects of a sort never seen in handmade spectacles, which often look flat. The so-called 'soft look' of 1972 exploited this to the full. From 1973 Christian Dior frames grew ever more colourful and more like jewellery; for instance, a frame-and-brooch combination with silver alloy chain was available. A promotional brochure from 1980 claims that Dior's optical frames and sunglasses intentionally followed (rather than led) fashion trends and that they were distributed internationally through a vast network of opticians. The spectacles demonstrated the House of Dior's attention to minute detail: materials, shapes and colours were researched 'as imaginatively as the fashion creation they accessorize. As a well-cut dress follows every movement of the body, Christian Dior glasses, ultra-light, adapt perfectly to facial contours.' Dior once said that 'in matters of elegance the detail is as important as the essential'. The use of enamelling and gemstones reinforced the luxury nature of the brand, and Christian Dior frames even enjoyed a hip-hop following in the late 1970s before those protagonists discovered Cazal (p. 131).

By 1982 the Optyl company was producing twelve new models a year for Dior, with the licensing authority in Paris commenting on styling and colours. Each model came in six colours and two sizes, whereas a more basic range, such as Optyl's Terri Brogan range, would be available in only three colours but many more sizes. In Britain, Harrods was selling Christian Dior in 1985 as a 'sophisticated' range; for example, a folding half-eye frame in nickel silver, plated with gold or chrome, sold for £90. In 1986 the company introduced a lizard-skin leather finish, widely reported as being crocodile and thus reviewed by one journalist as being 'combined with colours no crocodile ever wore', including frosted violet, blue and apricot. In 1987, on the occasion of the Christian Dior fortieth anniversary, Optyl's CEO, Harald Stolzenberg, was honoured with the Médaille de Vermeil from the city of Paris, demonstrating the gratitude that this so-French of brands felt towards its Austrian partners. By 1992 Gianfranco Ferré, whose own eponymous eyewear brand had been particularly big in the 1970s, was designer of haute couture for Dior. He introduced the monogram range featuring the five letters C, D, I, O and R interwoven on a bridge of gold (model 2640) or Optyl (model 2635). This was a conscious revival of a logo first seen on Dior gowns back in 1957.

In 1996 the Italian Safilo Group gained control of the Christian Dior brand through its purchase of the Carrera assets, and the brand has latterly been marketed as simply Dior. Shy celebrities, and those women who wish to emulate them, have favoured Dior's oversized 'windshields', such as the Aviadior (2006), described in company marketing as 'the must-have for the vintage soul'. In June 2005 *Vision 2020* magazine quoted Wilhelm Anger as saying that he believed that 'the agreement with Dior was a key step in elevating eyewear to a high-fashion accessory. In order to merchandise eyewear as an accessory, we needed branded names.' What he perhaps could not have predicted was how enduring that brand name would be, although of course an oft-quoted saying of Christian Dior is 'I shall hold firm.'

Christian Dior case, early 1990s.

Model 2346, late 1980s.

Model 2075 Monsieur men's reading spectacles (c. 1993) with sides of light-coated metal (LCM), as the brand calls its metal-coating process.

Cutler and Gross

In the world of British optometry (as opposed to dispensing opticians' practices or eyewear manufacturers/designers), fashion eyewear was not introduced from outside, but rather from within, although for years Graham Cutler and Tony Gross ploughed a lonely furrow, tolerated by their peers perhaps only because they operated on a small scale. The two met in 1960 while studying optics at London's Northampton College of Advanced Technology (now City University London), and in 1971 established an optical practice in London's upmarket Knightsbridge area. Despite international expansion the company has retained its base at this practice. Once very avant-garde, the brand is now noted also for its vintage collections.

Graham Cutler (born 1938) was prompted to train as an ophthalmic optician after working with the eye department of the Royal Air Force Medical Services during his national service. He was a researcher and part-time instructor in optics for a while, then joined the firm of Walters & Hillel, where he fitted hearing-aid spectacles. Cutler then branched out alone and tasted his true vocation during a brief collaboration designing some frames with Oliver Goldsmith (p. 49). The decision to go into business with Gross in 1969 owed as much to circumstances as it did to the desire for more excitement.

Tony Gross (born 1939) has been deemed, by himself among others, 'the mouth' in the partnership. He wrote in the foreword to his company's fortieth-anniversary book, *Forty Years of Vision and Style* (2009): 'In my time I was the best.' He went on to explain, no less modestly, how he overcame the prejudice of those who saw the fashion world as superficial and unbecoming for a serious professional. In the 1960s Gross took the view that everyone should aspire to look like a film star in glasses, himself favouring suits similar to those worn by French actor Jean Gabin. 'Everything in life', he said, 'must have sex appeal. Otherwise it is no good', and (when he was not busy serving as the house poker player at the White Elephant club) he drew inspiration for spectacle designs from his extensive personal collection of erotic literature and art books.

Cutler discovered the property at 16 Knightsbridge Green in late 1970. The shop was fitted out in 1971 by Piers Gough (it was one of the architect's earliest achievements)

Jarvis Cocker, who won fame as the frontman for the Britpop band Pulp, wearing Cutler and Gross eyewear in 2006.

OPPOSITE
A Cutler and Gross publicity shot from 2006.

and retained its distinctive, trendsetting look for more than thirty years until it was refurbished in a more modern style, with white walls and mirrors. Even then a memory of the past remained in the deep-red carpet of the same colour that Gough had specified.

Gross's brother, John, was at one time editor of the *Times Literary Supplement*, so he had ways and means of obtaining publicity, but above all it was the product (manufactured on-site) that made this no ordinary optical practice. Cutler and Gross became known as makers of handcrafted spectacle frames. They employed an old-time frame maker, George Smith, whom Gross lured from the firm of Ian Prince (see p. 14, top image), and designed frames for him to make. The frames were numerically named; the first, model 101, looked a bit like a Wayfarer from Ray-Ban (p. 67), but in crystal acetate. The firm has been known mainly for its acetate frames ever since, and has now passed frame number 1000. In contrast to, say, Silhouette (p. 103), Gross flatly refused to consider making rimless frames, claiming the firm was not in the business of making frames that pretended they weren't there. This is still Cutler and Gross policy.

For the first fifteen years the two partners would not supply frames whole-sale to other shops: customers had to buy directly from them. To walk through the Cutler and Gross door was a conscious decision, but one that increasing numbers of influential people took. Cutler and Gross made the spectacles, and its customers made the cult. In the 1970s the writer A.A. Gill paid £15 (a sum that was

1

2

3

1
Model 0207, mid-1980s.

2
The 0139 frame, one of a series commissioned by Cutler and Gross from outside factories from the mid-1980s. This model was produced in the Jura region of France on the same heating machine that had once been used to make 'bespoke' frames for Greek shipping magnate Aristotle Onassis.

3
A publicity shot from 2006.

4
A prototype for the metal aviator model 0269, 1992. Crosses on the lens mark the optical centre.

then equivalent to a week's food budget) for a pair of large black Cutler and Gross spectacles, justifying the extravagance in an essay entitled 'Four Eyes Only' with the remark 'But who needs to eat when you could look interesting and be fed?'

Cutler and Gross frames usually stem from a simple idea, and they have a whiff of spontaneity about them that derives from the fact that the designers could simply nip upstairs to get Smith to realize their ideas or to make minor adjustments to ideas already in progress, perhaps in response to a waiting client's wishes down in the shop. In the late 1970s Cutler and Gross opened a second London shop in collaboration with Anglo American (p. 27). The venture was not an economic success and the shop soon closed, but the brand continued to thrive,

4

Model 0205, *c.* 1990.
The typical Cutler and Gross
flat front makes these spectacles
look more obviously handmade.

with celebrity clients from the worlds of music (such as Bryan Ferry and Grace Jones) and the silver screen (such as Ava Gardner). Under designer Marie Wilkinson, appointed in 1982, the company was one of the very few British brands that exhibited at the French SILMO optical trade fair.

In 1984 Cutler and Gross started to commission individual factories to make certain frames off-site. Leather-covered frames sold well, as did those inspired by jewels, featuring faceted front and back surfaces. In 2001 the brand opened a vintage shop a few doors away from the main shop; its stock was originally based on Gross's personal historical collection, but frames from the main shop now transfer there after two years. Whereas some fashion houses refuse to remake old lines, Cutler and Gross has prospered by doing just that, whether of its own design or a competitor's. For instance, the vintage shop sold several examples of the oversized square-rimmed acetate frame Ultra Goliath, produced by Ultra Palm Optical, importer of Cazal (p. 131); this model inspired the 0851 model Cutler and Gross made in 2000 as part of a 'record collectors' collection, which proved a particular hit in Japan.

Under the direction of chief executive Majid Mohammadi, in 2007 Cutler and Gross opened a shop in Hong Kong in collaboration with Puyi Optical. The company now maintains its own factory in Cadore, Italy. Despite this expansion, Cutler and Gross's appeal is largely predicated on smallness of scale, Mohammadi being quoted in *The Times* as saying, 'When you are a true luxury brand you can't be big because then you are not exclusive.'

Elton John
Born Reginald Dwight (1947), English
singer-songwriter, composer and pianist

Elton John in concert in 2006. The eyewear is less flamboyant than in the past, but still unmistakably designer-style.

In a recording career that stretches back to 1968, Elton John has sold over 250 million records and has probably bought almost as many spectacle frames – give or take a few million.

Before his first concert in the United States in 1970 John went into well-known American optical store Lugene's and asked to go through the drawers of old stock, only to discover that the dispensing assistant, Lawrence Jenkin (see Anglo American, p. 27), had beaten him to it. On stage that same year John sported a pair with palm trees sprouting up from the outer rims, and soon his concert stage sets included an illuminated spectacle-shaped sign.

London's Victoria and Albert Museum has several of the star's spectacles in its theatre and performance collections, including a pair forming the shape of two beamed musical notes. The front cover of *Time* magazine's edition of 7 July 1975 featured an illustration of John wearing white plastic frames with lightning-flash lenses. Other styles he wore were the Star, the Flame, Stars and

Stripes (with EJ monogram in the corners), Mask, Feathers, Mouth and Bicycle.

Journalists delighted in comparing John's spectacle-wearing exploits with those of the American entertainer Sammy Davis Jr. One story had it that in 1977, after John had bought spectacles reported to be worth £9000, Davis determined to outdo his British rival, so bought a diamond-studded pair for £11,000; the following year John's then-manager, John Reid, bought the singer a pair of sunglasses (a real shell frame flown in from India, which he had inset with a raw diamond and an emerald) valued at £12,500.

As well as bespoke frames, John has enjoyed buying multiple models of various cult brands. In 2004 Cutler and Gross achieved a great publicity coup when John was featured in *Time Out London* magazine clutching one of its carrier bags and recommending the shop as a good source of Christmas presents.

With so many glasses in John's closet, it proved necessary to have a clear-out. An auction at

Sotheby's in 1988 featured more than sixty pairs, the first of which, a startlingly bright yellow frame by Silhouette (p. 103) glazed with yellow prescription lenses, sold for £1050 (Silhouette would go on to produce a special collection for John in 2000); another seven pairs went for the same amount, and the top price raised was £3200. The catalogue for this sale is now itself a collector's item. A further auction was announced in 2002, at which time it was reported that John owned 4000 pairs and had once admitted to having bought 20,000 over the years.

In 1995 the American eyewear manufacturer Oliver Peoples issued a limited-edition range in collaboration with the Elton John AIDS Foundation, and sunglasses have featured on the shelves of John's annual 'Out of the Closet' temporary shop sales in aid of his AIDS charity. In December 2009 John was widely quoted in the press as saying about these sales: 'I think the idea that the items we all buy and enjoy can help someone in dire need ... really strikes a chord.'

Lafont

P art of the attractive quality of Lafont is that the business retains much of the character of the small family firm from which it originated in the 1920s. If you stroll down the narrow rue Vignon in Paris's 8th *arrondissement* you still encounter the shopfront erected by Louis Lafont in 1923, and you can still peer into the basement workshop where the final preparation of prescriptions takes place and where, unusually, the prescription workers still work with gas flames. Historic advertisements displayed inside the shop show that the business began by selling both spectacles and hearing aids – evidence of a commercial diversity indicating that this seemingly very traditional firm was in fact ahead of its time – and although that particular product combination is no longer offered, the firm (which is still family-run) has continued to innovate.

The eyewear brand was originally named after Jean Lafont, who succeeded to his father's business in 1945, but it is named in tribute, for it was actually the third generation that redirected the company towards frame design. Philippe Lafont (born 1947), grandson of the founder, together with his wife, Laurence (1946–2008), first launched the Lunettes Jean Lafont range in 1971 and

The late Laurence Lafont, a designer whose husband, the grandson of the founder of Lafont, encouraged her to turn to eyewear in 1971, with great and colourful success. She also designed bedlinen and soft furnishings.

Lafont Paris shopfronts and interior, Paris (left and below).

OPPOSITE
Lafont cat's-eye frame as featured in the French magazine *Femme* in 1987.

In this 1970s acetate frame, a classic black was given some surface interest that also served to camouflage the pin covers.

An aviator sunglass frame from the 1970s, one of the earliest Lafont frames, demonstrates the designer's interest in colour. The frame is similar to that offered by several other manufacturers, apart from the fact that it has been sprayed green.

registered it as a brand two years later. Both were designers. Laurence also designed a folding lorgnette and, importantly for the continuity of the business, taught their son Thomas to design in the traditional manner: by drawing. This concentration on two-dimensional design means that many Lafont frames have a characteristic flatness. Lafont's famous Saigon frame of about 1990, inspired by oriental spectacles of more than a century earlier, is very flat indeed.

In the early years Laurence was the principal Lafont designer, taking classic shapes but experimenting with a far wider range of materials and, especially, colours than was the custom for the period. Lafont still likes to offer exclusive colours, even if it necessitates buying a full 100 kg (220 lb) of acetate sheet. At the time of writing 70 per cent of the colours on offer were exclusive, and the business employed a British colourist for this important role. One exclusive acetate colour, the Panther (no. 380) was available for some twenty-five years. Black acetate and 'shell' are, of course, not exclusive, and have featured continuously in the company's offerings. The early 1970s range reflected the style of twenty years earlier, including 'retro' vertical oval shapes. The typical French spectacle wearer at this time had a choice of five to ten brands at most, so a metropolitan-inspired 'exclusive' product was all the more noticeable. In the 1980s Lafont's acetate frames sold so well that they became, for a while, almost the company's sole product. In a classic 'rainbow' range of that decade, each style was available in one colour only, but each of those styles was in a different colour.

The original Lafont shop on rue Vignon still offers the vintage line. The modern range is sold in three other Lafont shops in Paris; these boutiques were opened from the late 1980s, concurrently with the company's international expansion via subsidiaries established in New York, Germany, Spain and Sweden. Lafont frames gained a high enough international profile that they were among the designer products mentioned by Bret Easton Ellis in his novel *American Psycho* (1991; see p. 123).

Naturally a city-centre workshop could not cope with this increase in production. Lafont became a design studio, which these days works from a warehouse in Issy-les-Moulineaux, south-west of Paris. There a small dog, Ginette (also referred to as the 'Vice Chairman'), roams the corridors, and the walls are stacked with museum guidebooks, books on design, travel brochures and fashion magazines – whatever might inspire the designer. An industrial partnership with the Thierry company in France's Jura mountains was set up in 1978, and this connection ensured that Lafont could not

Yan (*c.* 1975), in shell, has a vertical look accentuated by the high-placed bridge.

Andante (*c.* 1995), was a rare departure by Lafont into a rimless style.

Chichi (1999; below), is notable for its horizontally flat metal sides featuring a stamped-out pattern. As the firm explains, in France describing something as *chichi* means that it is overdone, fussy and contrived.

The Genie acetate frame (1980s), in imitation tortoiseshell with a classic keyhole bridge and high joints. It was Lafont's bestseller at the time.

Saigon (c. 1990, is today a very collectable frame. It recalls historic Chinese frames that featured flat bridges bearing a stylized cut-out pattern of a butterfly, symbolizing felicity – although the pinning arrangement is distinctly Western, and the colour scheme would never have been seen in the Orient.

Roxanne, Eyewear of the Year at Japan's IOFT trade fair in 2006, with a small splash of colour confined to the end covers.

Surprise, winner of the award for best sunglasses of the year at the French SILMO trade show in 2006. Laurence Lafont, the designer, loved lime-green and purple. These colours were not always popular for spectacle frames, but their inclusion in the range reinforced the firm's reputation for exclusive colours.

only operate on a commercial scale but also keep up with major changes in the industry.

The new millennium saw a resurgence of the brand as Thomas Lafont took the reins; from 2008 he also headed the design studio. Currently Lafont aims to produce a new collection every six months. In 2007 the firm, formerly (and, to a large extent, still) known for its traditional craft methods, employed new technology in the form of a chemical cutting process on the frame produced for the twentieth anniversary of the establishment of its American subsidiary; unusually, on this frame, the Twenty, the Lafont name is visible from the outside.

Whereas in France the company targets a broad market, in the United States it has aimed at the high end. Even in the early days Philippe Lafont wanted to sell outside France, and 70 per cent of sales now occur abroad, mostly in North America. In 2008 Lafont decided to expand its range of retro styles, and these now account for 20 per cent of the firm's custom. It is even possible to buy a bespoke shell frame from Lafont for about €8000 (about £6800), or a frame handmade on demand for a tenth of that price.

American Psycho

Psychological thriller written by Bret Easton Ellis (1991)

M-4XL by Oliver Peoples, 1990s. Oliver Peoples eyewear features in the novel *American Psycho*, as do models by Lafont and Ray-Ban.

At the start of his controversial novel, Bret Easton Ellis emphasizes his intention not 'to disparage any company's products' in his tale of the exploits of psychopathic Manhattan investment banker Patrick Bateman. Nevertheless, the book includes many references to horn-rimmed glasses as well as ultra-specific references to consumer products for wearing, grooming, entertaining and drinking.

Bateman assesses people he meets by the identifiable brands they are wearing; for instance, at Harry's bar he meets Luis Carruthers, who is wearing Oliver Peoples horn-rimmed glasses but is, in Bateman's opinion, 'not dressed well'. Another acquaintance, Preston, joins them: 'He takes off his glasses (Oliver Peoples of course) and yawns, wiping them clean with an Armani handkerchief.'

The original Oliver Peoples, dispensing opticians on the East coast of America, ceased trading in 1986 and left stock of over 1500 frames (many in 12-carat gold). This was bought by optician Larry Leight, his brother Dennis and childhood friend Kenny Schwartz, who opened the first Oliver Peoples store on Sunset Boulevard in Los Angeles later the same year. Early publicity for the brand was gained when Leight's fanciful design for Andy Warhol was featured on the cover of German *Vogue* in 1987, although the next major campaign, in 1988, placed the emphasis on the company's real 'working opticians'.

In *American Psycho*, we learn that in the street Bateman wears black Wayfarer aviator sunglasses (see Ray-Ban, p. 67) – the same as Tom Cruise, whom he meets in a lift. He also wears them at the office, while staring into his computer screen. He even pays $2000 at Bloomingdale's for a pair to give his hospitalized mother.

Despite the endorsement of Ray-Ban, Bateman wears his own Oliver Peoples (non-prescription) spectacles on a visit to the Paul Smith boutique. On a separate occasion, he and another man are in Harry's bar, each wearing a pair of spectacles by Lafont, one a pair of sunglasses, the other clear prescription eyeglasses (indeed, the obsessive Bateman notices whether or not a pair of spectacles is prescription; he can even spot redwood frames across a nightclub). Elsewhere in the novel the lowering of sunglasses, whatever the brand, takes on a dramatic turn more than once.

Oliver Peoples was a little-known brand in Britain in the early 1990s. In 1993 Angela Campbell, a dispensing optician who was frequently quoted in the British professional press for her willingness to source unusual brands, imported an Oliver Peoples combination frame because it resembled one worn by Denzel Washington in the film *Malcolm X* (1992). Significantly, the suggestion was not that the brand had actually been used in the film, merely that a customer would choose the Oliver Peoples style on the basis of its similarity.

Robert La Roche

R obert La Roche came late to eyewear, bringing with him the experienced eye of a general designer (a trade in which he was self-taught) and the insight of a marketing genius. His spectacles, though of mid-range price, had a carefully cultivated image, or 'aura', about them that made them seem far more expensive – which was exactly as he intended.

La Roche was born in 1938 in Vienna, Austria, but embarked on a career in marketing across Germany, the United States and Japan, mainly concerning himself with the food sector. He then returned to Austria and worked as an advertising manager for Optyl (see Viennaline/Serge Kirchhofer, p. 87), but – luckily, as he later saw it – was dismissed. He began designing his own eyewear, branded with his own name, in 1973. On showing his collection to a Viennese optician, he was asked: 'Are you an optician?' 'No,' he replied, 'I have a degree in economics.' 'I am sorry for you', came the response.* In the early years he was more successful in Innsbruck, where he was often received as 'the sales representative from Robert La Roche'. He was able to win some potential buyers over by being able to

Robert La Roche (above), founder of the brand.

S-73 sunglasses in plastic with metal trim, 1998 (above, left).

Model 349, c. 1985. Unlike the usual two-tone front, the 349's frame is plainer at the top. This was an experimental idea that Robert La Roche felt worked very successfully.

Model S-161 from the Optical Art range, 1997.

OPPOSITE
A monochrome publicity shot for Model S-68, 1998.

* From an interview with the author, February 2010.

Combo 7, 1987. La Roche always preferred to work in plastic. This combination frame, which was produced to use up plastic offcuts, became a hit with the wives of German opticians.

Mask, *c.* 1983–84. Robert La Roche fronts are sometimes cut in awkward shapes, but the reverse always has a normal, easily glazed shape.

Model 554, 1996. As with most Robert La Roche frames, branding appears only on the inside of the frame.

answer the design-related questions they occasionally put to him.

La Roche has always described opticians, somewhat ambiguously, as 'filters' between the brand and the eventual wearer. One such optician, Alain Mikli (p. 135), was his first representative in France, and l.a. Eyeworks (p. 139) was for a while his exclusive distributor in Los Angeles. The latter wanted him to design for them but were not prepared to feature his brand name. Early models were made for La Roche in Britain by Anglo American (p. 27), and later production was entrusted to the 'simplicity' of Italian spectacle makers, who were usually happy to discuss changes over the telephone. For ten years from 1988, La Roche held an exclusive licensing agreement with the Hoya Corporation of Japan, and he likes to tell the story of how he broke into the Japanese market by the simple expedient of agreeing to have his products manufactured there. As in the case of many eyewear designers, La Roche has also worked freelance, in his case for Essilor, designing Escada sunglasses for several years, and as a consultant for Calvin Klein Eyewear.

Robert La Roche spectacles have been seen as defining 'classic understatement' while at the same time being considered to be remarkably on trend with regard to colour and shape, and they also feature some interesting combinations of materials. New models came in up to twenty different colours. La Roche disliked metal, thinking it a 'cold' material, preferring imitation shell or horn. Already in the 1980s he favoured smaller rims than was common at the time, and in this sense he could be said to have anticipated the direction of fashion. Nevertheless, he produced frames that had a retro feel, willingly describing his output as *nouveau classique*.

Despite issuing more than fifty new designs a year by the late 1990s, La Roche used to boast of being the only eyewear manufacturer without a catalogue. His self-designed publicity material was geared instead to promoting the 'aura' of the brand, and he won awards for the quality of his advertising (much of which was produced in black and white, a format he claimed was 'aesthetically more exclusive'). Some frames included in the adverts were in fact never available commercially. And when a frame did go to market but was not successful, it all added to the 'aura', and La Roche was often amused to note that other companies would soon be selling something similar.

Notable La Roche advertising campaigns included double-page spreads in the 'in-crowd' American magazine *Interview*, co-founded by Andy Warhol. The choice of publication was important; at the time *Interview* had a circulation of only 100,000, but La Roche recognized that what would secure his brand's reputation was the nature of the readership rather than its quantity. Other companies, such as l.a. Eyeworks and Silhouette (p. 103), soon followed his

Model 13 from the Tweed Collection (1993), with appropriately patterned lugs intended to offer an 'English Lordly look'.

Model 658 with aluminium trim, *c.* 1995.

Model S-163 from the Optical Art Collection, 1997.

Model S-157, 1993.

1, 2, 3
Monochrome advertising
for the 649 model, 1998.

4
A photograph by
T. Popinger promoting the
Rob range launched in
1994, featuring a frame
with only one attached side.

5
Trendsetters, a rare
instance of a dated Robert
La Roche catalogue, 1991.

6
Model S-1001 (*c.* 1998–99),
one of the last Robert La
Roche styles to be designed
by La Roche himself.

7
From the Ichi-Ban
collection, 1993.

1

2

3

4

5

6

7

example. La Roche's Optical Art promotion of 1997 departed from the norm of photographing frames on faces. Instead, brochures showed frames dipped in water, distorted, or having milk poured over them. His promotional methods, as much as his product, were responsible for achieving yet further publicity.

Two other collections stand out in the comparatively short history of Robert La Roche: Rob and Ichi-Ban. Rob, launched in 1994, was a 'collection for young budgets', intended to retail at less than the psychologically significant price of 1000 schillings. La Roche has described these frames as having been 'knocked off' in response to cut-price frames being offered by the German chain of Fielmann. He did not skimp on the marketing campaign, however, and some of the photographs are notable for including dismantled frames. Ultimately this sub-collection did not succeed: opticians attempted to sell it at the same price as other Robert La Roche frames, and it also resulted in fewer of the more expensive frames being sold. Even so, La Roche won plaudits and environmental credibility among the young for packaging the range in paper bags rather than plastic pouches, and for his promotional materials made from corrugated cardboard.

Ichi-Ban (from the Japanese for 'first class' or 'number one') of 1993 was La Roche's first attempt to sell a complete package to opticians, and represented his love of Japan. He personally contacted forty-five of Austria's seven hundred or so opticians, offering them a set of frames to be presented on tatami mats, as well as small presentation tables and lacquerware boxes,

1

2

3

made in Japan, in which to display them. Every frame had an additional accessory of a pair of rimless clip-on sunglass lenses and a pouch featuring *netsuke* beads (traditional Japanese miniature carvings).

In 1999 La Roche retired (by which time much of the production of his spectacles had been outsourced to Austrian companies) and sold his trademark to Uniopt of Graz, but he has since designed the Onono range for ic! berlin (p. 161). In 2007 the Robert La Roche brand was relaunched under designers Alexandra Giselbrecht and Klaus Huber – a bold move, since, more than most, the brand had hitherto relied heavily on the personal qualities and attributes of the original designer.

4

5

1, 2, 3
Advertising of 1997–98, featuring (left to right) the S-72, 644 and 649 models.

4
Robert La Roche-branded spectacle cases.

5
Model S-76 (1998), offered in black or white.

Cazal

'Cassies' were for a while the undisputed eyewear of choice for the American hip-hop generation. This phenomenon was unintended by their German creator, and left him feeling uncomfortable. Conceived as sophisticated 'jewellery for the face', the brand (founded in 1975) instead entered the world of bling and, having now left that behind, it has continued to offer innovative designs. Nevertheless, its early frames, stamped 'Made in West Germany' – produced before unification – continue to excite the vintage-eyewear market.

The name Cazal derives from the first syllables of the designer's name, Cari Zalloni (born 1937). The aggressive styles designed by Zalloni (who also spent twelve years designing the Saphira range for Optyl; see Viennaline/Serge Kirchhofer, p. 87) are notable for their unique polygonal shapes, sometimes featuring deliberately sharp edges, and in the spring 2004 issue of *Sleaze* magazine he stated that 'A designer eyewear line that pleases everyone is unlikely to inspire. Good design must be thought-provoking.' Zalloni sketches all models, approves the pre-production samples and carries out regular checks at subsequent stages. At one point he regularly wore a Cazal 163, but he now says that his favourite design is always the next one.

By 1982 the Cazal range had grown to some fifty models, including the Targa sun frame with interchangeable solid- or graduated-tint lenses, which came with a case that had a special pocket to accommodate the spares. Despite Cazal's short production runs, the firm could still undertake to supply parts for any frame it had made since its foundation. Reflecting a conservative West German culture, sales representatives in that country were instructed to dress conservatively and drive Mercedes; there were no female representatives, in order to avoid disapproval from the opticians' wives. But Cazal quickly made the intelligent move of offering quite

Cazal founder and designer Cari Zalloni, wearing a Cazal 634, launched in 1988.

Cazal 163 (1985) shows how colourful 'Cassies' can be.

OPPOSITE
Original advertising for model 904, launched in 1986.

Cazal 961 (1993) with gold trim, branded sides and a frame that has been 'electro-coated', as the firm calls it. Polygonal rims were the height of fashion in the 1980s, but this pair from the British Optical Association Museum's collection may have belonged to an older customer, as suggested by the bifocal lenses. The Cazal brand dates from 1975; its frames were available in the United Kingdom from 1982.

All Cazal frames have begun as hand-drawn sketches by the company founder. The design shown below is for model 951 (1980s).

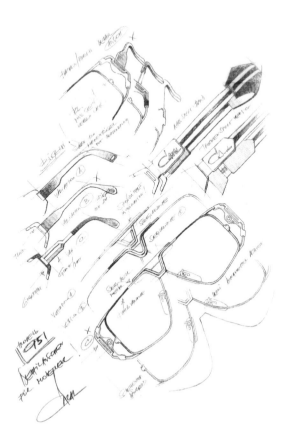

different styles to the American market, with frames in such bright colours as red and bedecked in precious stones, and a quite different consumer profile resulted.

In 1987 it was reported in the British professional press that 'In the last few years available production facilities at Cazal's Lower Bavarian town of Passau have not been able to meet demand, despite their being doubled.' Even before the company shifted manufacture to Munich it was producing half a million frames a year, and in the same reports the managing director, Herr Paetzold, stated, 'We are not fearful of competition, because our products sell to those who understand.'

In Cazal's 1980s hip-hop heyday the two cult frames were the 951 and its close relation, the 955. The 900 series of which they were a part was the most exclusive and expensive range, with typically large frames, often described as 'oversized'. Other models that were popular with 'b-boys' included the 821 and the 607, as worn by rap star Darryl 'DMC' McDaniels of the New York group Run-DMC. This group was hugely influential on the street-music and -fashion scene, and has been credited with

driving hip hop from its 'glam' origins in the 1970s into a more 'street' style. The Cazal 607 features numerous times in Jamel Shabazz's cult book documenting the 1980s hip-hop culture, *Back in the Days* (2001). Equipped with a camera, Shabazz took to the streets of Harlem, Queens and Brooklyn to capture 'the cool truth', and Cazal sunglasses emerge as an essential element of 'cool', even when worn with shop-display lenses announcing the brand name. The desire to wear was as important as the act of wearing: one photograph shows two brothers looking wistfully into the window of a spectacle shop.

The majority of that 1980s street generation could never have afforded such highly priced sunglasses, and to the designer's great distress Cazal frames became quite literally 'to die for', with some murders of young men in American cities being attributed to the theft of their Cazals. After the fatal stabbing in 1984 in Philadelphia of nineteen-year-old James Himmons, for instance, Britain's *Daily Mail* reported that his stolen Cazal frames, which cost some $500 new, would have been sold on for only a tiny fraction of that price. In 1985 a group calling themselves the Cazal Boys even wrote a song called 'Snatchin' Cazals', which consisted of six minutes of a refrain calling out the letters, 'the C-A-Z, the A and the L', and the warning 'You'll be dead before your time'.

More latterly Cazal has experimented with such materials as Monel (a nickel/copper alloy) overlaid with three layers of 24-carat-gold plating, and intricate finishes using China lacquer, which is much more costly than conventional enamelling. Cazal sometimes adds coloured foil, using a heat application process. The 652 acetate and Monel model, launched in 1999 as part of a new 'basic' range for men, was offered in three colour combinations: honey and blue, black and silver, and 'bordeaux' and antique gold. In 2003 the company introduced a notable advertising campaign featuring apparently naked models and the slogan 'Clothe your eyes'. Celebrities spotted in Cazals include MC Hammer (in the 858), Brad Pitt (in the 735), Beyoncé and Jay-Z (both in the 907).

Recently classic early Cazal models have been reissued, not without some measure of regret from Zalloni, who has bemoaned the fact that reissues do not require fresh design (although that is to ignore the subtle updating that has taken place, including the use of lighter materials and marginally smaller frame dimensions). The 2010 version of the 951 sports model, for example, now boasts plastic edging in the same colour as the lenses.

The Cazal 607 Sun (1977) was a particular hit among hip-hop fans. It was never officially introduced as a 'sun' version, rather the frame was individually fitted with sunglass lenses by the wearers. The 600 series also attracted Michael Jackson, who wore the 623 in his video for 'Bad' (1987). American entertainer Sammy Davis Jr also once wore a 623.

Model 990 (1999) is an example of a frame produced exclusively for the American market. Distributors included Eastern States Eyewear and Ultra Palm Optical.

The Nefertiti display head (far left) of 1993 was originally intended to display the 745 model, but here it shows a 202, a frame from 1976 with dark upper rim.

Model 728 (1986), a variation on the pilot style with a crossover bridge.

Alain Mikli

A Frenchman of Armenian origins, though born in Beirut, Alain Mikli (born 1955) is said by those who have met him to be as seductive as his luxury frames. Certainly the association between the man and his designs is one of the strongest in the industry, despite his success being predicated partly on numerous collaborations and on a most commendable initiative to promote the work of young designers. In his book *Spectacles: From Utility Article to Cult Object* (1998), Michael Andressen went so far as to describe Mikli as 'the father of modern glasses', hinting perhaps that his design output over more than thirty years has been almost promiscuous.

Mikli's output began precociously, too: Alain Miklitarian (his mother coined the shortened 'Mikli' name when he was a youth) moulded his first plastic frame aged just seventeen and established Mikli Diffusion in Paris in 1978, in his early twenties. His œuvre has been considered to be both provocative and eccentric. One French designer who has worked in Mikli's office has said that it was like working on another planet, but in nurturing the cult of the brand this sort of publicity is by no means harmful.

In April 1988 *The Optician* quoted Mikli as saying that his designs could take anything between five minutes and five months to complete, and that despite being a fully qualified optometrist he was now a full-time designer and had ceased to carry out sight tests. Some designs were retro-inspired, as was the case in 1989 when Mikli introduced a thick-rimmed round frame (reviewed in the *New York Times* as 'a modified John Lennon look is the newest old thing'). That same year *Optometry Today* stated that 'Alain Mikli sells mostly to people in show-business such as singers and actors. The extraordinary styles in this range sell to such personalities as Grace Jones and Jack Nicholson, and have price tags to match.'

Mikli's designs have sometimes been sharp and unsettling. This is exemplified by his – very successful – work produced from 1986 in collaboration with British designer Alyson Magee (who later became the first designer for the new Mikli Studio brand, established in 2005 with the explicit aim of supporting new designers branching out on their own). Together they made the eyewear for the apocalyptic film *Until the End of the World* (1991), directed by Wim Wenders. Mikli was asked to design eight

Alain Mikli (left), a precocious designer whose ideas sometimes pile up on top of one another (opposite). When asked by the editor of *The Optician* in 1987 where he got his ideas, Mikli replied, 'What shall I say today?'

OVERLEAF
A selection of frames produced by Mikli since 1978, clockwise from top centre: model 0116668 with protruding lashes; flamboyant model 054176; model 305101 Fleche, an asymmetric frame featuring an upward-pointing arrow; model 516632, with non-geometric outer rim; Lunette Main in the form of a pair of hands; model 5684-1025, studded like a belt, or even a dog collar; and model 4102-027, suspended from a bar.

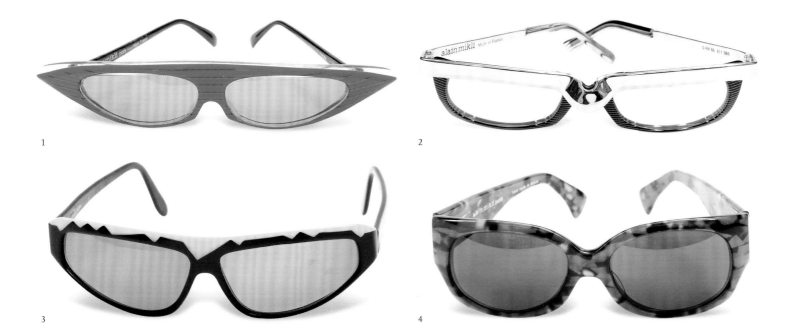

1

2

3

4

new styles for the film, and declared in the journal *Dispensing Optics* the year the film came out that he was 'very enthusiastic about this project as it gave [him] the chance to imagine styles of the near future'. Critics have suggested that Mikli did not really understand how best to exploit the publicity, but the fact remains that several of the outlandish, futuristic frames enjoyed commercial success, which is all the more remarkable since the film itself has not weathered well.

No mere props, the spectacles in *Until the End of the World* set the theme for a story that revolves around eyesight. In a sometimes muddled plot, set in 1999 but with fashions that at times seem to hark back more to the New Romantics of the early 1980s, William Hurt plays Sam Farber, the operator of a revolutionary camera designed by his ophthalmologist father to record dreams and restore vision to blind people. The featured technology was ahead of its time, anticipating, for example, satellite navi-gation, camera phones and congestion charging. The eyewear, which in the film is meant to offer protection in a post-nuclear wasteland, is notable for its thick sides reminiscent of safety glasses.

A remarkable side to Mikli's work has been his willingness to design for his competitors, concurrently with furthering his own brand – an increasingly common practice today, but one that he pioneered. He has designed Ray-Bans (p. 67) and Izzard for Sun Reeve of Japan, and co-signed frame ranges with Philippe Starck and Issey Miyake; his collaboration with the latter, which began in the late 1990s, is best known for the Dragonfly frame (2001), which folded away into a case resembling a cocoon.

Mikli's frames have been worth the attention of criminal copyists, and he has been prominent in the campaign against counterfeiting of designer goods, going so far as to arrange for frames to be seized from competitors' stands at the Italian MIDO trade fair.

5

6

1
Model 0104 (1984) features a green laminate triangular rim on crystal that contrasts with the sinister black sides.

2
Model 611 (1986) is notable for its inclined front, which recalls, if not intentionally, nineteenth-century pantoscopic spectacles.

3
Neige des Montagnes ('mountain snow') frame (model 316, 1986) with 'snow' covering the upper rim surface. This black-and-yellow version proves that in a designer's mind snow does not need to be white. Early to mid-1980s frames by Mikli are easy to date, as they feature a two-digit number on the inner side.

4
Model 3180 (date unknown), with thick red-and-black sides.

5, 6
Two of the frames designed for the film *Until the End of the World* (1991).

l.a. Eyeworks

Barbara McReynolds (born 1946), one of the co-founders of the American optical practice l.a. Eyeworks, had always been intrigued by spectacles, and, aged twelve, tricked an optometrist into prescribing her first pair. Her future friend and partner Gai Gherardi (born 1946) had a similar compulsion, donning an eye patch to visit the doctor; she has recalled that she was driven by a desire to wear big round glasses. In 1979, by then both experienced opticians, the two were joined by Margo Willits (born 1950) to open a shop on Melrose Avenue in Los Angeles.

The partners sought to react against the prevailing trend for brand logos, oversized rims and (as they saw it) the bland colour range of Optyl, and the gender expectations of the time whereby women were supposed to wear one thing (gigantic and overwrought) and men another (also big, but grey/brown and 'boring'). They accordingly started selling such smaller, archetypal frames as stock-issue American military and British NHS-type spectacles – including the almost medicinal, pink crystal Pennington frame from American Optical (p. 23). The next step was to adapt and customize their stock, taking, for example, the Nusir frame by

The Beat (1980). The model was issued in five colour families.

OPPOSITE
Andy Warhol in the L.A.X frame, photographed for an l.a. Eyeworks campaign in 1985.

Shuron in an unpopular but neutral colour called Moon Seed and transforming it through a regime of hand-dyeing and sand-blasting. This had the additional result of rendering the frames gender-neutral. They found it liberating to put the same frame on a man and a woman, and see a transformation on both.

In about 1980, having been unsuccessful in convincing Bausch & Lomb that it should make the Ray-Ban Wayfarer (see p. 67) in additional colours, McReynolds and Gherardi visited Britain and mainland Europe to learn how frames were made. They greatly admired the Speedway frame by Gaspari and the work of Dora Demmel at Silhouette (p. 103). In Paris, at the Printemps department store, the partners were stunned by a frame by Alain Mikli (p. 135), who was relatively unknown in the United States at the time, and identified him as a kindred soul; they sought him out and bought his entire collection. When this sold out after their return to Los Angeles, they ordered the entire collection again. Although these experiences informed their design thinking, McReynolds and Gherardi were equally inspired by many things that had nothing to do with eyewear, 'be it

Leonard Cohen, Vivienne Westwood, Antoni Gaudí, surf culture, or whatever. We just knew there was another frame design paradigm out there waiting to be born.'*

Since they were so dissatisfied with the way frame fashion had evolved, McReynolds and Gherardi began deliberately swimming upstream with their first own-brand design, the Beat, in 1980. With this unisex acetate frame, which had a hand-treated finish, the designers made an affectionate nod to the surf culture of their native Huntington Beach. The success of the Beat, which they ended up making in more than a hundred colours, was a revelation. For the designers, it was as surprising as it was inspiring that the enthusiasm increased as they pushed the proposition further with Botta (1983), a combination frame offered in arresting primary colours, and then Gigantor (1986), another combination frame but one that met the 1980s passion for geometrical shaping in its exaggerated brow and daring dimensions.

In 1992 *International Design Magazine* awarded l.a. Eyeworks a gold medal for product design in recognition of 'the long-standing creative spirit of the company'. Even though the partners had never really

dared to hope for such plaudits, one thing they had hoped would succeed was to take manufacturing to 'amazing craftspeople' at idle factories in less developed countries. They tried production in a number of places, including Morocco and the former Czechoslovakia, but to their regret, this wasn't entirely viable.

At Melrose Avenue l.a. Eyeworks created a gallery context where the frames were presented sparingly and repetitively. It was so unlike a normal optical practice that the shop was used in the science-fiction film *Blade Runner* (1982) as the location for the futuristic dispensary for replicant eyes. Subsequently the shop window was used as a means with which to hold 'conversations with the street'; for the first ten years Gherardi was responsible for this, but contributions were then invited from guest artists, notably Jim Reva, and Robert Warner, who curated a window in which spectacle frames were hung in condoms, along with the giant slogan 'Safe spex'.

Gherardi claims that the brand's marketing image was 'inspired by the diverse beauty of the faces at that time'. To be on Melrose Avenue in 1980 was to be at the heart of the punk movement, with its Mohawk haircuts and elaborate fashions. The New Wave movement followed, with its audacious colour and geometry. Both trends reopened the face for celebration and spawned various company slogans, including 'Facing the change/Changing the face', which adorned full-page advertisements in such 'in-crowd' publications as *Interview*.

Since 1982 l.a. Eyeworks' most notable campaign has declared, 'A face is like a work of art. It deserves a great frame.'

From the Pluto series of 1987: (top to bottom) Models III, I and II.

Bodhi (left) and Luck (bottom), with clips, both from 1994. These frames have been among l.a. Eyeworks' most successful commercially. The designers have admitted that they were startled to find their instincts about the small, metal-rimmed Bodhi so enthusiastically confirmed.

Examples from the Bondo series, one of l.a. Eyeworks' most 'cult' ranges. From top: Bondito (1996), Bondo (1990) and James Bondo (1996). Bondo features twenty-six individual solder points.

The colourful Radar collection, launched at the French SILMO trade fair in 2005. Its visible rivets gave it a distinctly retro feel.

This long-running, mostly black-and-white portrait campaign was conceived by McReynolds and Gherardi's friends and customers Gary Johns and Jeff Gorman, who worked for the advertising firm Chiat/Day and had recently won acclaim for their work for Nike. It was Johns who suggested that l.a. Eyeworks simply celebrate the amazing faces all around them in black-and-white photographs, and Gorman who conceived the tag line. The original intention was to divide the portrait shoots among emerging young photographers. However, after Matthew Rolston took the first two, McReynolds and Gherardi worked with Gorman on the third and knew they had found a very special kinship; Gorman's work has been an indelible part of the l.a. Eyeworks signature for the three decades since that time, featuring such celebrities as Arnold Schwarzenegger, Sharon Stone, Divine, RuPaul and Lenny Kravitz. Gorman's book, *Inside Life* (1996), includes many of his photographs from these campaigns.

The l.a. Eyeworks portrait campaign, however, was primarily about honouring faces, and emerged from a kind of naïve innocence. Belinda Carlisle, the second face photographed (Levi Dexter was the first), was a customer. McReynolds has recalled: 'We simply suggested that we'd love to photograph her and she agreed. In terms of rights, permissions, agents and management, it was a much different time. We acted on impulse.'

XOX (1991), a Love and Kisses frame featuring laser-cut letters.

Tiny Matters (1995), a limited-edition miniature frame inscribed on the inside with 'Stop narrow minds'. The frame, the front of which measures just 85 mm (3 3/8 in.) wide by 23 mm (7/8 in.) high, was produced as a gift for wholesale customers and friends in the optical industry who 'complete the thought' in l.a. Eyeworks' representation of the brand. The small frame was intended to remind people that small things matter and deserve attention.

U-Turn (2004), in laser-etched acetate, broke the rules by occluding part of the outer edge of the lens.

Reverse of the Stop Watch All the Time (1994), another frame produced as a gift.

Police

Always an arresting sight, Police sunglasses and ophthalmic frames make up one of the best-known male fashion eyewear collections. In the 1990s they were the subject of a remarkable series of celebrity-endorsed promotional campaigns; even more remarkably, the brand subsequently abandoned that approach in favour of a celebration of its customers, using 'ordinary' people to feature in its advertisements.

Police, launched in 1983, was the first in-house brand of the Italian frame manufacturer De Rigo. The firm would later go on to acquire the long-established Italian brand Lozza, as well as the licensing rights for, among others, Givenchy and Chopard. It also ensured widespread distribution through the ambitious acquisition of major chains of high-street opticians, notably Dollond & Aitchison in Britain, General Optica in Spain and Portugal, and Opmar Optik in Turkey.

Police frames have been produced at a factory in Longarone, north-eastern Italy, since 1995, and are now sold in more than eighty countries. By 2008, the brand's silver jubilee year, Police had become a global lifestyle brand that included clothing and

These women (far left), from a Police advertisement of 1989, demonstrate the wider appeal of what was an essentially masculine range. Model 2051's one-piece lens and bridge section depends on the full-width upper bar and provides all the more surface on which to reflect the cityscape.

Police designer Bruno Palmegiani (left).

The Vogart 2131 from 1986 (below), showing Police's pre-2005 spread-eagle logo on the front lug and the brand name spelled out on the side's outer surface.

OPPOSITE
A Police advert from 1983–84, with metropolitan New York background. The powerful young man has, of course, a strong woman beside him.

The Vogart 1001, a classic Police square aviator with the two-part rim and blue lens that have become synonymous with the brand. Dating from 1988, the style was relaunched in 2010.

accessories produced in association with a number of licence partners, featuring black leather jackets and related 'urban' gear.

Police began life as a self-consciously masculine eyewear brand. Early advertising emphasized the metropolitan background of New York City, and although the frames were designed for men, they were shown being worn by both sexes. Bruno Palmegiani, designer for De Rigo, wanted to target the young or youthfully minded urban spirit. He aimed to produce a transatlantic tribe of Police 'addicts', and the brand's distinctive combination of blue lenses (introduced in 1993) and gold frames used across all international markets represents an early example for eyewear of commercial globalization. The original brand logo, the spread eagle, represented a new freedom of vision across borders (on some styles the eagle's wings spread from the joints across the edge of the lens); in about 2005 the logo was changed to a Gothic letter P.

The Police brand gained renown for its marketing campaigns featuring top international icons from the worlds of film and sport. The company labelled these celebrities 'spokespersons'. All were male, but the aim was to attract both sexes; they would

be sex symbols for women and role models for men. Each spokesperson offered a different charisma, but in each instance he was portrayed against a common metropolitan 'Police' background.

From 1998 the campaign was headed by the Italian footballer Paolo Maldini, who debuted for AC Milan in 1985 and for the national team in 1988 (Maldini went on to become the grand old man of the game, retiring aged forty in 2009 as Italy's most capped player). From 1999 to 2001 the face of Police was the actor Bruce Willis, representing strength, courage and the irreverent, raw hero; perhaps not coincidentally, he had played the role of policeman in several films, notably the *Die Hard* series. Willis was followed (from 2002 to 2003) by George Clooney, who, in contrast to his predecessor, was selected to represent intelligence, seduction and class – qualities he was felt to embody in his role as Dr Doug Ross in the television hospital drama *ER*, which first aired in 1994. His place in the international campaign was taken by David Beckham (see p. 149), who had already been promoting the brand in certain territories for three years. Antonio Banderas, portrayer of Zorro, the masked crime

Model 2147 (*c.* 1993–94) combined blue lenses with the contrasting yellow of a gold frame. Eagle wings spread out from the edges of the bridge, and the motif is repeated at the joints.

Model 2181 (left; launched 1994), with winged upper bridge, a motif repeated on the half-covered sides. The bowed bridge on model 2194 (far left; also 1994) has winged ends, and the brand name is spelled out in letters.

Model 2278 (1996) featured notched edges to the lower bridge and sides, which gave a masculine, industrial feel to the sunglasses and appealed to its target audience.

1
Models 2182 (men's) and 2192 as advertised in 1994. Note the changed form of the eagle logo. The iconic blue lens formed the main image for that year's collection.

2
George Clooney, Police 'spokesperson' from 2002 to 2003, was perceived as being as cool at the operating table as at the pool table.

3
Bruce Willis, photographed for Police by Uli Weber in 1999.

4
The Italian footballer Paolo Maldini was selected to advertise Police sunglasses in 1998 for his athletic allure. Claudio Pagan's photographs brought out a relaxed, fun-loving figure.

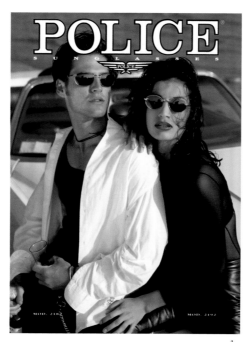

1

2

3

4

fighter (and actually the son of a policeman), fronted the campaign from 2007; photographed by Carlo Miari Fulcis, he oozed the passion and sex appeal of the timeless Latin lover. By this time De Rigo was explicitly promoting the Police spectacle frame as a cult object: 'They transform the wearer into an icon, the consumption of an image.'

It was around this time that the phrase 'Be Younique' was first used in Police advertising, and in 2008 De Rigo announced a radical turning point in its communication strategy: 'Police has decided to trust to the taste and personality of its most loyal customers and to rely on their ability to stand out as fashion lovers, and not as fashion victims, through their personal and unique lifestyles.' The brand's image makers set off on a hunt to identify 'street' personalities rendered 'younique' by their striking qualities, passions and occupations (the last including a shark dentist, an elephant-sitter and a shampoo tester).

The 'Be Younique' campaign was developed by the 1861 United agency of Milan, and was shot on the streets of New York by the portraitist Pierpaolo Ferrari. An annual competition to appoint a complete unknown as the face of the brand was first won (in 2009) by Andrea Garbolino, a nineteen-year-old Italian architecture student. The conventional press was largely shunned in favour of a dedicated website and digital screen advertising in city centres.

David Beckham
(born 1975) English footballer

David Beckham sported several different hairstyles during his time promoting Police. The 2005 campaign introduced the use of gothic script and the single letter P as a logo on the frame.

David Beckham was the international face of Police from 2004 to 2006. Although he was born to a humble east London family, he fitted the American New York image perfectly; he even named his first son Brooklyn. Beckham debuted for Manchester United in 1992, and England in 1996. He later played abroad for Real Madrid (2003–2007), and then for Los Angeles Galaxy from 2007. Beckham's marriage in 1999 to 'Posh Spice' of 'girl band' the Spice Girls, Victoria Adams, contributed to his celebrity beyond football.

Before endorsing Police, Beckham had already appeared on marketing material for eyewear (but not bespectacled), for the Manchester United official eyewear collection launched in 1999 by Pennine Optical, but that had been a relatively small campaign. Police employed a triple marketing approach, using press, posters and cinema, and, in a pioneering promotional activity, also showed these advertisements in discotheques.

When Beckham was selected for Police's international campaign, he had already been used to promote the brand in England and Japan for several years. In 2000, when Beckham was named as the new 'local' face of Police (for which he was paid a six-figure sum), the UK managing director announced: 'We wanted to link up with David Beckham because he uniquely combines extraordinary fashion and style with unsurpassed passion and individualism.'

In his autobiography *My World* (2000), Beckham wondered: 'How can people be so interested in us [the Beckham couple] that it's front page news if we go shopping, wear something different or get our hair cut?' Elsewhere in the book he claimed: 'I watch fashion programmes sometimes and look through magazines but I'm not that influenced by them. If I see something I like, I get it whether or not it's in fashion.' On another page, however, he admitted to having more

clothes than Victoria, and a bigger wardrobe.

Beckham appeared in British marketing campaigns for Police from March 2001. The new Police range launched in London that spring was one of the major attractions at Optrafair, where it was stated in the official catalogue that 'De Rigo has had a phenomenal amount of interest with orders exceeding all expectations for the collection which comprises 23 new models including the DB range designed for the footballer (model numbers 2663, 2646 and 2678)'.

In 2002 Beckham was hailed as the ultimate 'metrosexual' by British writer and broadcaster Mark Simpson – who invented the term – in an article in salon.com, the online magazine, specifically mentioning the footballer's endorsement of Police sunglasses; sarong-wearing Beckham has been described as such by many other writers since.

theo

In 1984 English optometrist Claude Lyons wrote a letter to the *Ophthalmic Optician* relating a friend's correspondence from Belgium: 'They all promote very fancy frames ... of all sorts and colours ... No one admits to buying inexpensive frames ... In fact everyone seems to delight in boasting how much they paid for their specs. The opticians here must make a fortune.' In 1987 theo was established by two such fortune-seeking Belgian opticians, Wim Somers (born 1950) and Patrick Hoet (born 1952); the brand's name, an anagram of Hoet's surname, was chosen because it is easily pronounced in many languages. The original motto was 'Do not just see better, also look better', but it is now, simply, 'theo loves you'.

Somers has said that his only aim when he opened his Somers Optiek store on the Eiermarkt in Antwerp in 1980 was to be different from everyone else. Thus he stocked frames by Robert La Roche (p. 125), Oliver Peoples (he was one of the first to do so; see p. 123) and Alain Mikli (p. 135). Students from the nearby fashion academy often asked him for frames to use in their catwalk shows, and invited him along as a guest. Hoet, who owned an optical store in

Company founders Wim Somers (far left), wearing a theo soixante5, and Patrick Hoet wearing a PA model from eye-witness (2007), a sister brand to theo that was launched in 1994.

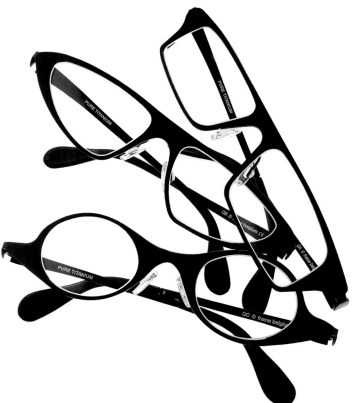

With the 'morphologically asymmetrical' eye-witness line, Hoet enjoyed more design freedom than with the theo collection. The frames may appear to be unfinished, but Hoet regards symmetry as a 'facile' solution. The spectacles are eye-catching, but the brand philosophy is that they still need to be chosen to suit the individual's face (which may, of course, be far from symmetrical).

OPPOSITE
The Wim frame (2006), part of the Designer collection, named after Antwerp fashion clothing designer Wim Neels.

1

2

1

Brainwear (1999) was an unusual frame on a headband, reminiscent of the *spina frontalis* style made in continental Europe in the late eighteenth century. As the company puts it: 'A pair of theo glasses underlines the personality of the wearer, it does not define it.'

2

From the Satisfashion range, 2001–2003.

3

Mele, the longest-lived theo frame, launched in 2000. The frame is horizontally flat but has a projecting bridge that rests on the nose in a lower position than is the norm. Some 10,000 pairs of the frame were sold in the United States, where Microsoft's Bill Gates was one purchaser of the model.

4

Moby Dick, from the Wrasse range of 2004 made in collaboration with young German fashion designer Christoph Broich. The range's distinctive feature is the safety-pin design, which was expensive to produce; this model, which was worn by actress Kim Cattrall in the film *Sex and the City*, featured an extra-large pin. Part of the design idea was that women could wear these sunglasses easily on top of their heads.

3

4

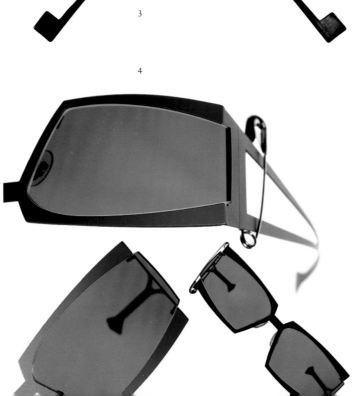

Bruges, designed exclusively for theo and its sister brand, eye-witness, for more than twenty years, until he began his own line in parallel in 2008. He has always designed by hand, starting with an idea and then working it out; the eye-witness range is distinctive for its deliberate if sometimes subtle asymmetry.

Today theo retails across fifty countries, but in the early days the brand was followed by only a very limited group of avant-garde people. Many people outside Belgium didn't know where Antwerp was, or even where Belgium was. At first the business supplied just four opticians, three of whom are still involved; one of them, Alain Bekaert, is still the international sales representative.

At theo's first trade show, the French SILMO in 1989, three hundred frames were sold 'guerilla-style' on the stairs. Notable early theo frames are of buffalo horn. Subsequently the double-layered front has come to typify the brand; the two layers can be coloured separately, as in the Tarot models of about 2005. The Designer collection of 2006 combined stainless steel

1

1
The theo by Tim Van Steenbergen range has decorative screw heads embedded in the end covers of the sides. The Belgian fashion designer's frames have won notice for their notably wide sides near the joints and the fenestrations in the rims.

2
Franklin-type double lenses – lenses divided into two halves, as originally associated with the eighteenth-century American scientist and statesman Benjamin Franklin – are one of theo's favourite design ideas. Every year the firm includes some in the new range. The BiCycle frame (2009) pictured here was intended for artists and other creative types.

3
The Bruges Lace and Antwerp Mesh models were launched at the Italian MIDO trade fair in 2005, and then exhibited at the World Fair in Japan. Mesh ties in with the old port industry of the brand's home city and is more masculine than the chemically etched Lace. It won the French Silmo d'Or award in 2006 for 'most extravagant sunglasses'. The firm has also won prizes in the United States and Japan.

4
The Sthereo range (2010) from the Soixante collection came in black acetate with rivet covers reminiscent of control icons on modern CD and DVD players, and featured fluorescent inlays so that wearers could be seen in the dark. Only 100 pieces of each model were produced.

2

3

4

Hesperia Comma (top) and Limenitis Reducta (bottom), from the Tim Van Steenbergen collection, *c*. 2009.

From the Hats collection (2010; far right), named after various other items of headgear, including the Trilby, Borsalino, Gatsby, Panama and Stetson, made of Monel with bronze metal sides. The frame runs uninterrupted around both lenses. There are humorous flourishes, for instance where the metal side tip meets the plastic end cover.

Caline (2007), a 'special' frame intended as a collectors' item and featuring a face 'veil' in gold, silver or black.

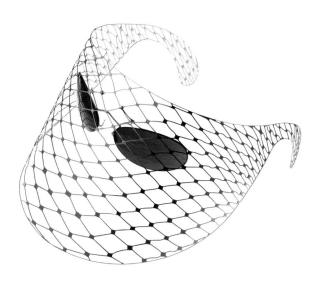

with plastic. Today's theo frames are mainly laser-cut from stainless steel.

Pleased to play the underdog, theo has tried not to be too commercial and has understated its achievements. Recent corporate publicity declared: 'The many prizes theo has won show that the theo approach is not a bad one.' Preferring to tackle new challenges rather than to maintain a winning formula, the company has seldom produced even its successful ranges (for instance, the award-winning Satisfashion sunglasses collection launched in 2001) for more than three years. The longest-lasting theo frame, Mele, was supplied for ten years before being withdrawn in 2009.

The theo brand has always supported the arts: each year the company sponsors a fashion student at Antwerp's Royal Academy of Fine Arts, and it has its own art gallery, which is run as a free space for artists (around the corner from its company base in a former barrel factory). In 2008 theo began working with Belgian fashion designer Tim Van Steenbergen, whose spectacles feature a signature detail of two parallel lines on the outside of the frame – hinting at his working method developed through working with drapery, building

a piece layer by layer – and his name on the inside.

Despite being run by opticians, theo concentrates its design work on appearance, not performance. The company is not averse to back-to-basics collections, such as its T.O. collection of 2004: 'sober and light with just that little of a theo aura around it'. It also issues regular limited editions, such as the Styl-O (2006) and the Caline (2007); only seventy-five of each were produced, in gold, silver and black, and they were supplied with a signed card in a special box. The Dauphinois model (2010), from the Potatoes range, featured horizontally flat sides, with a lighter colour on the top surface. This was theo's first departure into flexible sides and featured a visible spring; it took seven or eight attempts to get it right.

For its twentieth anniversary, in 2007, theo launched the Vingtage collection, the name and its spelling playing on the French word for 'twenty'. The design focus had shifted somewhat, from the eyes to the full face – that is, away from theo's traditional small-rimmed glasses to larger eye shapes. Although the brand used vintage styling, it resisted the temptation to remake old styles. Somers claims that he and Hoet 'added

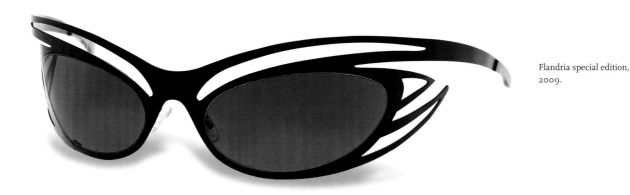

Flandria special edition,
2009.

'Designer spin':
a promotional image
showing various theo
ranges available in 2006.

more', such as surface decoration and colouring, than, say, a retro specialist firm such as Cutler and Gross (p. 113) would have done. The Vingtage range was produced mostly in metal but in shapes echoing those more usually found in plastic frames. Vingtage Soixante (2010), however, was theo's first acetate range; coloured details give the illusion of rivets. For the 2009 special edition, Flandria, Hoet took the functional shape of a bicycle racing helmet and added 'value' to it so that it could be worn on the street rather than in a race. Flandria was not intended for the sports eyewear market; rather, it was meant for people who wanted to stand out and thus 'beat the others'.

J.F. Rey

Jean-François Rey (born 1950) has been designing spectacles since his school holidays in the late 1960s, although his eponymous brand, inspired by primitive cultures and the natural world, is relatively new. It was perhaps inevitable that Rey, who was born in the French Jura region to parents who worked in the spectacle industry, would embark on a career in spectacle design. Yet it was not in his native region but in the far south of France that he and his wife, Joelle, would find their designer's idyll.

Some English-speaking opticians pronounce the brand name 'Jeffrey', almost as if the brand were a close friend with whom they are on first-name terms. In fact, the man behind the brand is known for his private discretion and quiet elegance. This is almost at odds with the commercial strapline that his frames are for people 'who don't want to hide, who are proud to be different'.

Different his frames certainly are. An enthusiast for Japanese style, Rey came to prominence in the early 1980s designing sunglasses for Issey Miyake. He went on to found and direct the IDC company, which began making sunglasses in about 1984 and then diversified into ophthalmic frames, and which became popular with a certain

type of British customer, such as graphic designers and architects, who bought them on trips to France. They lapped up Rey's wide oblong styles, which were designed in an atmosphere that Rey has since fondly recalled as 'liberating disregard'. He separated from his IDC associates in 1991 and the firm was liquidated. (It was later re-created, with no connection to Rey, as EyeDC.)

Rey's feminine Boz range, which launched in 1991 and immediately won the Silmo d'Or award, drew on his love of Asian culture, using ethnic prints, exotic graphic emblems, vegetable reliefs, floral patterns and even dried flowers, on openwork sides. Recent marketing literature has stated that it 'attracts women who like to seduce and create an energetic and colourful look for themselves'. This acts as a useful reminder that designers may work on more than just their own-name range, and, in considering Rey's achievements, it is also important to recognize the input of Joelle, who has been both a driving force behind Boz and her husband's principal colourist for all ranges.

Until now Rey's main input has been into the frame shape and the interplay between form and function. He has particularly enjoyed tackling the way the sides

Jean-François Rey, the firm's founder and designer, and his wife, Joelle, the principal colourist.

OPPOSITE
A promotional image for the JF2314, launched in 2009.

IDC 876 368, a shallow eye frame designed in about 1985 by Jean-François Rey for IDC, his first company.

J.F. Rey's JF2331 (2010), a rimless style with colourful three-dimensional springy sides that are almost divorced from the lenses.

JF2180, introduced in 2005, had lattice-effect sides and centrally attached lenses that splay out to the edges, away from the metal rims, in a form intended to suggest the gills of a fish.

connect to the front. The Genius frame, which won the French Silmo d'Or award in 2005, featured a one-piece steel front that transitioned into an acetate side with the smoothness of a twirling ribbon.

If Boz is exotic, the J.F. Rey brand has been described as more 'urban'. It stems from Rey's company BLI DBP, which he founded in the southern port city of Marseilles in 1992; although the brand is unisex, the emphasis is on the men's range, which accounts for at least 60 per cent of the business. Rey's first personal collection was launched in 1995, and, having taken off in North America and Japan, was introduced in Britain in 2007. The inspiration is the Mediterranean, which the designer sees every day from his studio, observing

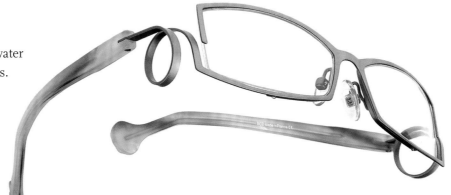

the way light reflects off the water in ever-changing colours. Whereas this view is, of course, unavailable to everyone not within reach of the French Riviera, the frames are marketed as very personal things to the customer: they are *Vos lunettes simplement* – 'Simply your glasses'.

The innovative Superflex range of 2009 (models JF2290, 2291 and 2292) featured the thinnest steel ever used in the optical field; because of their unusually long dimensions when folded, they had their own special cases. J.F. Rey sees such creativity as the brand's trademark, and so there are no oversized logos. Indeed, the absence of logos from the frames is trumpeted, for it leaves a larger area for decoration.

The Skyeyes acetate sunglass collection (introduced in 1999), another joint creation of husband and wife, aimed with a hint of irony at so-called 'fashion victims' and included retro styles targeting the male customer. In 2010 the couple unveiled a range of 1950s-inspired frames with inset semi-precious stones, and, unusually, these were used on male as well as female designs. Most extravagant of all is the entirely feminine Luxe Fleur d'Or (2008) from the Boz range; this solid-gold frame with diamonds was conceived in collaboration with the jeweller Roger Lebenstein, and retailed at €17,000 (about £14,000). The frame was in tune with an increasingly upmarket business direction that witnessed the opening of J.F. Rey boutiques in Paris, Tours and Tokyo.

The award-winning Genius (2005) from the Boz range carried the two-tone colouring right round the loops of the ribbon. It was all the more complicated to manufacture because the colour was applied after the twirling loop had been created.

The limited-edition Luxe Fleur d'Or of 2008 (left). The Kaprisse (far left) from the Boz range, which won the French Silmo d'Or in 2007, featured floral motifs in laser-cut stainless steel that seemed to grow around the glasses.

A model from the unisex Stones range, 2010.

ic! berlin

The exclamation mark in ic! berlin is justified by the firm winning Japan's IOFT Glasses of the Year award no fewer than four times between 1999 and 2005. The story began with a unique innovation in product design and progressed, despite the break-up of the original business partners, into a remarkable marketing phenomenon centred largely on one man. Despite issuing a frame called, simply, cult (the company has a tradition of starting its model names with lower-case letters), the German firm denies it is a cult, describing itself as a way of life.

The one man is Ralph Anderl (born 1970). In 1996 Anderl, who was studying for a doctorate (destined never to be completed), had what his friends Harald Gottschling and Philipp Haffmans were seeking: a photogenic bald head. Gottschling and Haffmans were both graduates of Berlin's University of the Arts and had designed spectacle frames for student competitions. On to Anderl's head they placed an experimental pair of sheet-aluminium spectacles featuring their embryonic version of a revolutionary screwless joint. The three partners set up what was little more than a 'living-room

ic! berlin's Ralph Anderl (left and opposite) in a 2005 promotion for the Onono range.

The company's first frame, jack (1998).

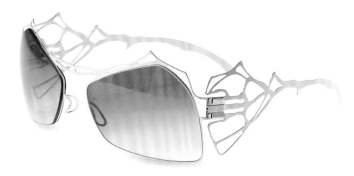

The druna frame (2002) exemplifies how the optical trade shows were enlivened by ic! berlin in the late 1990s and early 2000s.

Cult eyewear: this frame, actually called 'cult', was part of the Superfine collection (2006–2007) produced by London designers. The sub-collection Superlovers featured a frame inspired by country star Johnny Cash, and king, inspired by Elvis Presley.

ic! berlin is known for its regular special editions, such as the sakura (2006).

The adlerbrille 9615 (2007).

company' (in German, a *Wohnzimmerfirma*), which they called hga after their initials.

Having failed to interest an established manufacturer, the partners discovered in Hanover a technique for cutting sheets of stainless steel. The joint developed into a sprung-hinge insert system, and at an event in Berlin's Design-Transfer Gallery they presented their model, jack. People could buy vouchers at the event and received their frame three months later. Having persuaded German actors Corinna Harfouch and Peter Lohmeyer to wear their spectacles, the partners offered a debut collection at the Optica Cologne trade fair, where they came to the attention of Alain Mikli (p. 135), Robert La Roche (p. 125) and Danish frame designer Poul-Jorn Lindberg (see p. 17, bottom image). This networking paid off: at Italy's MIDO trade show in 1998, it was to La Roche's stand that they fled after they had been caught 'illegally' selling on the staircase. Later that year they walked away with the French Silmo d'Or award.

Only in 1999 did the partners establish a proper company, ic! berlin brillen. Early models included peggy, juri, max and phil p. The opticians they supplied had persuaded them to introduce a fastening clip so that the frames could be opened easily for reglazing. As the original joint was in two halves, it was protected from twisting by an S-curve (later used for the brand logo). Moritz Krueger joined the firm in 2001 as an apprentice, and had risen to sales manager by 2003. With his input ic! berlin opened twenty fashion accounts worldwide. The principal product had now taken a settled form, utilizing highly flexible

The model named after the brand: the eye c (2007). The frames may be technologically innovative, but they are not beyond comprehension by the customer. Each frame is supplied with instructions on assembling sheet-metal glasses, so that customers can change the lenses themselves, without the need for tools.

The mikame (2007), from the Plastic! collection, with a notable S-curve to the joint. Another model in the range was called 'nameless'.

The jeremy range from 2008 was designed by a new young member of staff. The various models were named after his relatives, including maman, papa, and soeur (sister). Shown here is grand-mère (grandmother); the young lad's grandmother even came to a trade show to help sell the frame.

The vendredi (Friday) frame from the très chic range (2008) was intended to enable a diva to end her week in style.

Robert 04 (right) and Robert 06 (below), both from the Onono range of 2008. The attention to the smart packaging reflects the input of Robert La Roche, who worked on this collection.

Urban (2008), from the Rx collection.

stainless steel, just 0.5 mm thick, acid-cut to shape and adjustable to all shapes of head. In 2003 Daniel Haffmans joined the business, having already worked for ic! berlin via his multimedia agency, and developed the company's corporate identity and communication strategy. But later that year four partners left to form Mykita (p. 167), leaving Anderl, the 'sheet-metal glasses salesman', to go it alone.

Berlin has been described as one of the most exciting cities of the early twenty-first century, and it was Anderl's good fortune to have both an entrepreneurial talent and

a dynamic urban environment in which to operate. Although the initial metal cutting is carried out in Italy, the frames are otherwise built from scratch in Berlin and hand-finished on the firm's premises – an old bakery with rooftop views from which one really can say 'I See Berlin!' Metaphorically and literally, this building is, as the company marketing literature claims, 'a platform for the realization of exciting ideas, simplicity, clarity and brilliant ingenuity'. The company aims to attract new artistic ideas and has been known to exchange a spectacle frame for a work of art from a local creative type.

ic! berlin has also worked with international designers. In Berlin these have included F.M. Hofmann (head of design), Thomas Bischoff, Antonia Kapretz and Bernhard Schwarzbauer, and designs have also been commissioned from Wolfgang Proksch in southern Germany, Arik Levi in Paris, Markus Moser in Zurich and Simon Koening in Basel, as well as a growing number of London-based designers, including Markus Lupfer, and Lucy Pinter and Flora Evans (who were behind the Superfine collection in 2006–2007).

At the Italian MIDO trade fair in 2005 ic! berlin launched its first non-metal collection, Plastic!, which featured acetate fronts combined with steel sides. The hinge was attached to the front with two-piece clips, involving no glue or embedding of any sort. While retaining the brand's basic simplicity, this collection opened the door to a greater use of colour and three-dimensional design than had been offered hitherto. Anderl claimed that the beauty of the frames was self-explanatory, entailing just three com-

ponents: front, side and two-piece clip (or sleeve). At that year's SILMO French trade show, ic! berlin launched a luxury horn brand, Onono, offering only twelve frames each year. In a classic promotional photoshoot for the range, Anderl gradually shaved his beard and head a little bit more for each image. In another marketing campaign, Anderl allowed himself to be wrapped bondage-style. That may not be a daily activity for every ic! berlin customer, but it did serve to attract attention to a brand that the proprietor hopes will 'evolve into a friend and close partner, a daily companion' for each customer.

Although unashamedly a self-publicist, Anderl took a back seat in 2008 as the company's female staff, led by Christina Muthsam, designed a collection by women for women, inspired by 1960s and 1970s Hollywood, under the name très chic. The range had as slogan 'Every day a diva', and the frames were named, in French, after the days of the week (there was also a silken sleeping mask for the weekend). Characteristically for the brand, Muthsam, a model and stylist as well as a designer, put herself at the forefront of the marketing imagery.

The frère frame from the jeremy collection of 2008.

Ralph Anderl in 'bondage' for a marketing campaign in 2010.

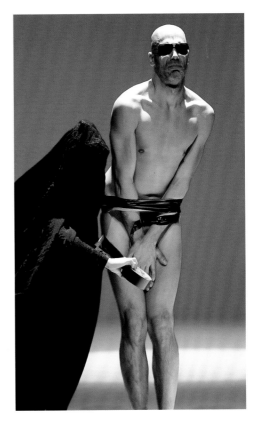

Mykita

The origins of Mykita lie in the story of ic! berlin, the company from which the founders split in 2003 (p. 161). Mykita took the same innovative product, but developed its own cult by placing the emphasis on construction rather than styling. Mykita frames are 'Handmade in Berlin' (or the Czech Republic), but in such a manner that they appear to have been manufactured on a computer-controlled automatic production line. Despite this, it would still be possible to claim (as the marketing director does) that 'It's like something your grandad would wear.'

Mykita was formed in Berlin in 2003 by Harald Gottschling (born 1968), Daniel Haffmans (born 1971), Philipp Haffmans (born 1968) and Moritz Krueger (born 1979). The company was named after its initial premises in a former children's day-care centre (*Kindertagesstätte* in German, usually abbreviated to *Kita* in the former East Germany), and a corporate culture arose that exploited this heritage. Mykita staff went to work 'to play with the face', as it were, and ate their midday meal together, helping the team to bond. Each Mykita model was to be named after a different fictitious child who might have attended the

The Dries frame (top), from Collection No.2, launched in 2006, and Chuck (left), from Mykita's first collection in 2004.

Mykita's founders (below, left to right): Philipp Haffmans, Harald Gottschling, Daniel Haffmans and Moritz Krueger.

OPPOSITE
Emmanuelle, 2010.

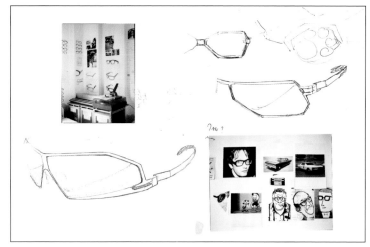

Sketch drawings for the Laika model and (below) the finished product, from Mykita's first collection, launched in 2004.

Rolf, from Collection No. 1, in 'goldline' with a gradient tint, encapsulates the macho style of the brand's first years.

Marcello, also from the first collection, was issued in a gold tartan pattern.

Kita; a few names have been obviously German, such as Bernhard, Helmut and Otto, but others have included Oliver, Nigel and David, Brooke, Roxanne and Brad, Giovanni and Isabella. Coincidentally, Mykita also means 'those who came from the north' in Japanese – which isn't particularly significant but does make the brand easier to promote in Far Eastern markets.

At the time of writing Mykita had issued just two main collections, both intended to last rather than enjoy the success of a one-season wonder. This approach can almost be seen as a self-conscious attempt not to be fashionable, and distinguishes the company markedly from the large fashion houses. Collection No. 1, launched at the French SILMO trade fair in 2004, was claimed to be 'an evolutionary step up in terms of both design and exclusivity'. The folded Scandinavian steel-sheet frames were remarkably light and could be easily configured by various adjustments to the interlocking components in order to fit the most strangely shaped face. The open manner in which the treatment of the material is displayed has been termed 'industrial aesthetic', and Mykita frames have been compared somewhat grandly with engravings by German Renaissance artist Albrecht Dürer. They look as though they have been cut by laser, but they have also been engraved with the precision of the early modern woodcut.

Mykita's Collection No. 1 did not feature many colours (so that it would not date too quickly), and certain models were deliberately targeted at specific demographics: the relatively shallow rectangular shape of Nils, for instance, was designed with

Erik, in 'silverline', from Collection No. 1. The Mykita Lite range of which it is part, featuring shapes reminiscent of the 1960s and 1970s with aviator and teardrop lens shapes, was characterized by its Swedish names.

the serious businessman in mind. The bestselling model in Collection No. 1 has been the Rolf aviator frame, a classic shape but realized in flat metal; fans of the brand feel that it almost merges into the face. It has proved popular with such celebrities as Brad Pitt, Angelina Jolie and Hugh Grant. Gradually the collection, encompassing both optical and sunglass frames, was expanded and more colours have been offered, such that the company could claim to offer 'a frame for every face'. At SILMO 2005 Mykita launched a further six sunglass frames and eleven optical frames. The sunglasses boasted an innovative 'silverline' finish on the material, featuring subtle engraved lines passing horizontally across the surface.

Not until 2006 did Mykita launch Collection No. 2 (although it did not discontinue the first). In a marked departure, this new collection featured frames made from acetate, but they retained distinctive sheath hinges that revealed a clear relationship with their steel predecessors. Nine colours were offered. Mykita won a Silmo d'Or award in 2007.

The first Mykita shop opened in Berlin in 2007, with a startling white interior that glowed like the moon in the dark. The theme has been continued at the company's trade-show stands, which have resembled an art gallery, consisting of a white box that the delegate must enter, and which are very relaxing inside. The brand campaign for 2010 was directed, as others before it had been, by the British artist and fashion photographer Mark Borthwick, who featured his friends and family, either in his own house or in Prospect Park, Brooklyn, and employed no artificial light, make-up or styling. The idea was that the publicity material shows the viewer how the spectacles would really look.

Promotional photography by Mark Borthwick, 2010.

RVS by V

When a young Turkish entrepreneur from outside the traditional centres of spectacle making developed a range of handcrafted sunglasses inspired by vintage styles, his brand's inclusion in this book became justified on the basis that it might represent a way forward for the niche side of the industry – although the suggestion is necessarily speculative.

RVS by V is self-consciously historical in its approach. Vidal Erkohen began as a collector of vintage sunglasses, notably Ray-Ban (p. 67), Carrera (p. 77) and Persol (p. 45). Born in New York in 1981, he was brought up in Turkey from the age of eleven but returned to New York to study fine arts at the city's Long Island University. He established his business (the initialism stands for 'Rare Vintage Sunglasses') in Istanbul in 2004. At the time the Turkish capital had become quite a centre for vintage clothing and accessories, with a number of boutiques and stalls in the city's Beyoğlu district, and RVS soon supplied to boutiques worldwide, including, among other places, in New York, Los Angeles, Brisbane, Tokyo, Lisbon and Stockholm. Eventually Erkohen decided to design his own range, which would pay homage to

RVS by V's founder and designer, Vidal Erkohen.

Robin (2009), a wraparound frame in grey and cobalt blue, with modern lines but recalling the historical 'mask' style. It was promoted with the tag line that it would 'bring out the hero in you'.

Luce (2008), a flat-topped frame in imitation shell and red acetate.

OPPOSITE
A promotional photograph for the RVS collection for spring 2008.

Morro (2008), a bold design in orange and imitation mottled shell, demonstrates RVS by V's distinctive matt finish. Real tortoiseshell would traditionally have been highly polished and would require constant repolishing to prevent the material disintegrating. Classic design features include the quadra eye shape, the revealed horizontal pinning and the keyhole bridge. RVS by V's eyewear is exported from the ancient merchant trading centre of Istanbul in little wooden crates (below) that declare the hand-craftsmanship of the twenty-first-century brand.

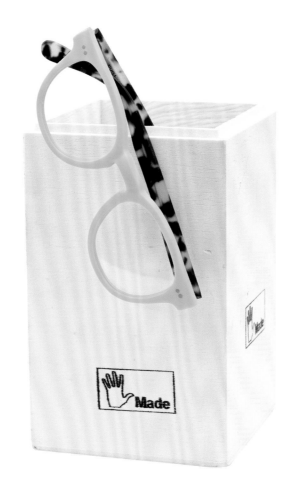

vintage quality and classic style. In 2006 he produced a provisional set of twenty-five pieces based on his first model, Naomi. The range was introduced to the market under the RVS by V brand the following year. Erkohen now offers spectacle frames made from high-quality Mazzucchelli acetate, with the challenge to customers to 'look at the future from within the quality of the past'.

RVS by V has since introduced four to five new models twice a year, in March and September, usually making at most 150 pieces of each model in various custom colours; it also makes occasional 'one-of-a-kind' pieces. As the frames are made piece by piece, only about 1500 can be produced each year. RVS by V frames are remarkably traditional-looking, as seen in their flat fronts. Aidan (2009), the company's smaller take on traditional aviator frames, had a fenestration above the flat bridge, in effect creating an impression of a browbar. The hand-cut and hand-polished nature of the frames is immediately visible, suggesting a roughness that larger brands might have wished to smooth away, at the expense of losing all sense of character. Aviva, also from 2009, was a remarkably old-fashioned folding model with hinges at the bridge and halfway along the sides, but in a modern palette of colours; another folding model from the same year is Air.

For the seriously historically minded customer, RVS by V's Phantom (2006–2007) and Zazie (2009) were both round-eye frames with shapes, if not finishes, that resembled frames from before there was such a thing as fashion eyewear: the first was pumped up in size, whereas the second was almost nineteenth-century in scale, being just large enough to cover the eyes. The front of the Maya frame (2008) was a classic metal–acetate combination style from the 1950s, but the differently coloured sides ensured that there could be no mistaken identity. Noah's ark supposedly came to rest in Turkey, and the company's Noah frame (2008), produced in one of the world's most ancient of cities, had thick 'library' sides that were almost antediluvian in appearance – but again the combination of different colours for front and sides gave it a decidedly modern look.

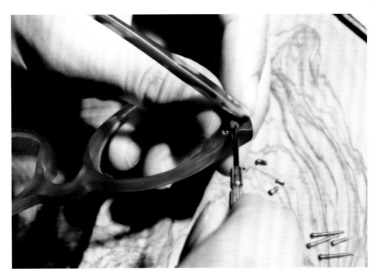

Reader (2009), a remarkable frame with an eye of just 39mm (1⁹⁄₁₆ in.), featuring a cobalt blue front with arch bridge and rigid pads in the same plane. Centre joints are embedded in the sinuous lugs. The reinforced drop-end sides are in an ultra-modern colour finish described as 'white ice'.

Inserting a screw by hand (left). RVS by V is noted for its hand-painted red screws, which provide a memorable brand identifier. The screw head is shown below, protruding from a triple charnier joint.

TD Tom Davies

Englishman Tom Davies (born 1974) has pioneered the idea of customer-driven bespoke design, while reviving a hands-on role in the creative process for the high-street optician. Future collectors of eyewear will enjoy the bonus of knowing the name of the original owner of each pair, because it is marked on the inner right side.

Introduced in Britain in 2007, TD Tom Davies frames are 'designed for you by your optician in collaboration with Tom Davies'. These opticians are trained at a two-day 'Design School' during which they are taught the use of a multi-layered computer program called Supertool. The opticians choose how many layers of customization to offer, and may reach expert levels. Customers come to them 'to buy their opinion', that is, to pay for the practitioners' advice.

The supervised TD Tom Davies design process utilizes a system that divides the face geometrically, as well as a further range of dispensing equipment that includes no fewer than forty-seven nose-fitting frames. At the end of the process the customer is usually presented with a choice of three frames superimposed on a portrait photograph. The selected frame is then ordered from a factory in Shenzhen, China. In 2010

acetate frames could be turned around in three weeks and titanium in four weeks.

Shenzhen was once merely a centre for mass production, but Davies sought out the best craftsmanship in the city and came to justify the use of his Chinese factory on grounds of quality, not just cost (although he is open about his ultimate desire to manufacture his favourite frames, titanium combination styles, in Japan). The company motto is 'Why compromise?', and the product has been praised as 'quality beyond reproach' by *Esquire* magazine. By the end of 2009 more than 1000 bespoke frames a month were being supplied. At that time of year Davies was expecting bespoke orders to slow down, so he designed 150 new frames for his ready-to-wear range, ready to slot into the quiet period of production. But bespoke did not slow down! Thus, although the *Financial Times* called the frames 'the most exclusive glasses in the world', there is a sense in which the bespoke service is becoming a mainstream phenomenon; in other words, a widespread cult.

Davies lists his hobby on YouTube as simply 'spectacles'. He admits that Alain Mikli (p. 135) was an influence, but he has striven to avoid copying, claiming that his

Tom Davies.

OPPOSITE
A worker crafting a bespoke frame by hand in the TD Tom Davies factory in China.

Every Tom Davies bespoke frame features the name of the person for whom it was made. Right, spectacles made for this book's author, featuring a retro combination frame softened by narrower styling and modern scratch finish. Below, a frame made for Johnny Depp.

Clients of TD Tom Davies frames can choose from an unusually wide range of colours, available across all styles.

main influence is the user. He studied film and television at the University of East Anglia before flying to China with his backpack in 1997 to work for a start-up eyewear factory. Thus cutting his teeth on the factory floor, Davies helped to build production from scratch while also designing for other international brands, including Fossil, Seiko and Puma. He returned to London in 2000 and set up a couture frame business, creating spectacles and sunglasses for such film stars as Rowan Atkinson (in *Keeping Mum*, 2005) and Kevin Spacey (in *Fred Claus*, 2007).

Even at £5000 a frame, Davies's waiting list sometimes ran to twelve months. He started with just one department-store outlet (at Harrods, naturally), where he met the customers personally. In the first year his turnover for couture frames was around £240,000, and it was at that stage that he was featured in the *Financial Times*. He immediately closed all his business with other brands.

By now Davies was dealing with about thirty opticians, a sufficiently small number that he was still able to present a personal service. One day a customer at his Selfridges outlet wanted to modify a frame. Davies's prototypes, which were produced abroad, cost around $40 to make, and he realized that, if only he had his own factory, he could make actual finished frames more cheaply than that. That was when he decided to set up a ready-to-wear line, which was offered through top international boutique opticians. In 2008 Davies opened his own factory in the hills outside Hong Kong (although he feels the word 'factory' is too industrial, preferring the term 'workshop').

TD Tom Davies frames are the result of an integration of the skills required for handmade craft with an automated ordering process. The frames are cut by machine to an accuracy of a tenth of a millimetre, then by way of initial polishing they are tumbled in revolving barrels for three days (one day less than the industry average, because over-tumbling leads to soft edges). As befits an Asian workshop, the tumbler is filled with bamboo. Then there is the hand-polishing: each frame experiences a total of about forty minutes of polishing by hand, as opposed to ten minutes in most of the eyewear industry.

A notable feature of the brand is the sandblasted scratch finish. On his blog in 2009 Davies recalled: 'It was a complete accident actually. Someone was trimming down some acetate with a wire brush and I thought it looked rather nice. So I had them do this to my sunglasses.' He does not really favour spring joints, regarding them as a substitute for a good fit, and the early products of the brand do not feature them. But in response to bespoke customer demand he then designed his distinctive T-joint (T for Tom). The brand also offers a distinctive pressure joint.

Davies considers his frames to be towards the high end of the market, but still accessible to customers who want an input in the final appearance of their eyewear. Each frame's end price is driven by the quality desired by the client, in consultation with their optician, the 'chief designer'. In the 'Design School' training video Davies does claim, however, that 'We make the best-quality frames in the world.' History will be the judge of that.

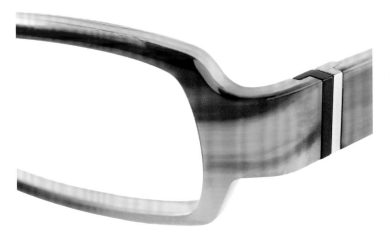

Even the TD T-joint can carry the brand identity.

A bespoke measuring frame.

A red women's acetate frame with keyhole bridge, high joints and reinforced sides.

This acetate frame mostly conveys a traditional male look, but features decidedly modern rectangular pin covers.

Ready-to-wear model TD0154 (2009) featuring a blue version of the distinctive TD pressure joint, which comprises a two-band metal spring rather than a hinge. The perfect fit is assured every time.

The Optical Trade Shows

The prestigious Silmo d'Or trophy, awarded at the French SILMO trade fair.

Glamorous models wearing glamorous frames have long been a staple part of the trade-show diet. Below are an image from the 1970s and (bottom) one from the 2000s.

To those who have enjoyed the artistry of the fashion shows organized by the Information Council of the Optical Industry in which the latest designs of spectacle frames may be seen worn jauntily by the elegant models, a visit to the Paris collections must have come as something of a shock. Whether it was a gimmick, or whatever you like to call it, the fact remains that when the Nina Ricci collection was shown all the models wore completely round Harold Lloyd type of spectacles, painted to match their outfits. Perhaps it was a subtle type of propaganda inspired by the contact lens manufacturers.

Ophthalmic Optician,
24 February 1962

Trade shows feature prominently in this book because they are the venues for product launches, the sponsors of industry awards and the means by which the spectacle industry divides its year. It has been argued by some that fashion in spectacles began in 1925, when Jules Monneret, principal of the technical college of Morez in eastern France, requested a stand at the International Exhibition of Decorative Arts in Paris, saying that he wanted to part French women from their disfiguring spectacles. Others, though, point to a fair dedicated to the subject held in 1913 in Turin, organized by Giuseppe Ratti, founder of Persol (p. 45).

Today's main French optical trade fair is SILMO (Salon International de la Lunetterie, de l'Optique Oculaire et du Matériel pour Opticiens). In 1964 two dozen spectacle makers from Oyonnax, in eastern France, exhibited at the Salon International des Plastiques held in their town, but the first 'proper' SILMO was held in 1967 as part of a wider optical trade show in purpose-built premises, with seventy exhibitors, nine of them from abroad (although the name SILMO was adopted only in 1970). SILMO was held in Paris for the first time in 1972, and thereafter the show alternated between Paris and Oyonnax every four years (except in 1980, when it was held in Lyon). Since 1981 it has been held yearly, in Paris. SILMO has built a reputation as the show with the greatest emphasis on spectacle frames, as opposed to, say, lenses or ophthalmic instrumentation. In 1997 it introduced a sports eyewear section and its Silmo d'Or award for innovation, technology and creativity, regarded as the industry's Oscars.

SILMO's Italian rival, MIDO, held in Milan, was established by a group of businessmen in 1970, building on the success of earlier shows held since 1967. Already by 1975 it was attracting 10,000 visitors, and it has grown into the largest of the fairs. It is regarded as the principal showcase for new ideas in frames on account of its Trend area, which was introduced in 1998 and later spawned an associated pubication, the *Fashion Trendbook*. In 1999 MIDO organizers claimed that there were as many as 140,000 new styles of sunglasses and frames on show, and by 2010 the claim was that more than 2 million models had been displayed by some 1500 brands.

In Germany, the major event for many years was Optica, held from the mid-1970s in Wiesbaden, Stuttgart and, most commonly, Cologne. In the early 1990s Cologne was seen as the ideal location because 130 million consumers – at the time, more than a third of the population of the European Community – lived within a radius of 500 kilometres (some 300 miles). By 2002, however, Optica was in trouble (it has now not been held for many years), principally owing to the success of a rival fair, Opti-Munich (originally called Opti-Mum), established in 1998 in Munich, an ideal meeting centre for opticians from Germany, Austria, Switzerland, Italy and the Czech Republic. Opti-Munich captured the spectacles zeitgeist, attracting such big names as Alain Mikli (p. 135), Filos, Marcolin and Marchon, and seemed to benefit from its January timing – the claim was that opticians liked to be able to buy as soon as the New Year began.

In 1947 W.E. Hardy, editor of British journal *The Optician*, co-organized with Swiss optometrist Ernst Lienberger the first post-war European optical fair, in Bern, Switzerland. In Britain itself, during the 1950s and 1960s the Information Council for the Optical Industry held regular displays for the public, featuring frames of unusual materials, including leather, canvas and bamboo. The British Ophthalmic Trade Fair held at London's Royal Albert Hall in 1961 featured fashion parades and a demonstration of hairstyling and glasses 'for ladies only'. In 1967 the first of several exhibitions was held at the Italian Trade Centre in London, featuring such brands as Filos, Correna,

Ratti-Meflecto (Persol, see p. 45), Cremona, Eidon, Safilo, Marcolin and Sferoflex. It was reported that 'the overall impression was that the Italians still have much to show us when it comes to style. Many of the frames were beautifully proportioned, obviously designed for their aesthetic appeal as well as their function.' Britain's optical trade show, Optrafair, is considered to have first been held in 1970 (although not under that name), and it has been set in Birmingham since 1982. In the late 1990s Kirk Originals (p. 39) was the driving force behind the first London International Optics (LIO) show, which attempted to push the fashion brands to the fore; l.a. Eyeworks (p. 139) and Oliver Peoples (p. 123) attended from the United States, but the number of delegates was too small to justify a repeat.

Today the American optical trade shows are aimed mostly at opticians, but thirty years ago they were targeted more at the agents and distributors, and companies often had two separate booths, the one for the opticians being smaller or less prominently situated; in the 1980s theo's Wim Somers (see p. 151) found it a real effort to source American brands for his Belgian practice. In the United States trade shows tended to be combined with professional conferences. For example, Optical Fair '72, in St Louis, Missouri, celebrated the seventy-fifth anniversary of the American Optometric Association, and in 1990 Optifair was incorporated

within the International Vision Expo & Conference West at Anaheim, California. Because of the country's large size there have necessarily been regional shows, such as Vision Expo East (VEE) and Vision Expo West (VEW).

Japan's first international optical trade fair was the IOFT in Tokyo, held in 1988 and organized by the Japan Medical-Optical Equipment Industrial Association.

A delegates' folder for the American Optifair. The last Optifair was held in 1989, after which it was succeeded by Vision Expo.

A booklet for the Italian MIDO fair, 2010.

A computer-designed trade-show stand for France's SILMO, 2009.

An eyewear fashion show at a mid-1970s trade event.

A frame from the Custom RUBIK-O brand of user-customizable eyewear manufactured from injection-moulded carbon fibre by FOVS of Italy, launched at MIDO 2010 in the Italian national colours.

Glossary

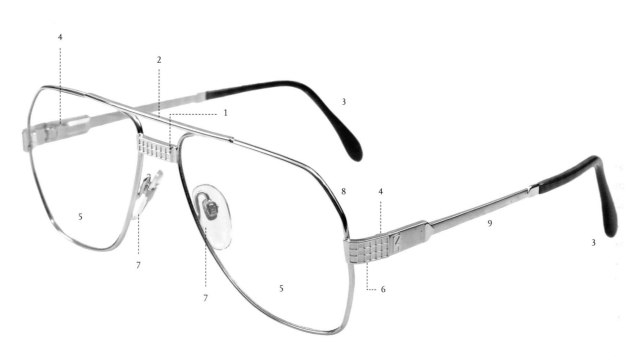

1 - Bridge

2 - Browbar

3 - End

4 - Joint

5 - Lens

6 - Lug

7 - Pad

8 - Rim

9 - Side

Aviator frame

Frame featuring a keyhole bridge

Terminology used throughout the book usually conforms to the British Standards Institute (BSI) nomenclature for spectacle frames, although occasionally some alternative terms have been used, such as 'glasses' (for 'spectacles') and 'temples' (for 'sides'), which are in very wide use and, in some countries, may even be the preferred terms.

The relevant British and European standard for the measurement of spectacle frames is BS EN ISO 8624:2002.

acetate: A popular plastic frame material noted for its strength and versatility, first produced commercially in 1914 and common by about 1930. Early acetate was more brittle than »nitrate and held colours less well, but was less irritating to the skin and lasted better in the long term (although no one predicted that when it was first developed). Acetate could be prepared in an »extrusion process from the early 1950s, allowing more elaborate colour designs to be achieved. *See also* »propionate.

aviator frame: A form of twentieth-century spectacle frame of a design based originally on pilot's goggles, which fitted snugly over the whole eye socket. Aviators are usually, if not always, made of metal with a prominent »browbar, a flat upper »rim contour and rounded lower rims covering a large portion of the face.

barrelling: A method of polishing spectacle frames by machine. Plastic »fronts and »sides are treated separately in (usually) a four-stage process from rough tumbling in barrels of birch pegs through to glossing in a barrel with pegs and smoothing oil. Each stage of the process typically lasts a day. Metal frames are commonly barrelled in their assembled form, using walnut granules before electroplating, or with steel ball-bearings either before or after that process.

block method: The traditional method for producing plain or patterned plastic sheets from which spectacle frames might be cut, first employed around 1880 to reproduce the appearance of »tortoiseshell. The material is formed as a gelatinous block that is then sliced, and the sheets are hung to harden. The block method was overtaken by the »extrusion process in the third quarter of the twentieth century, but has more recently found renewed favour.

bridge [1]: The connection between two »rims. Historic types include the C-shaped arch, X-bridge, K-bridge and W-bridge, the last introduced in the 1880s and popular well into the twentieth century. Bridges may be bowed, crested or inclined, decorated or plain. Common types today include pad, regular (without pads), saddle, and key form/keyhole (pictured above). The bridge may rest on the nose or be raised above it by pads. A bridge is often designed in association with a »browbar, forming, in effect, a double bridge. The reverse of metal bridges is a common place to engrave the brand or frame details, particularly the gold content of gold-filled frames, expressed as a percentage.

browbar [2]: A straight bar running across the top of a (usually metal) spectacle frame, along the browline above the bridge, connecting the upper »rims.

CE mark: Since 1992, spectacle frames made in the European Community (now the European Union) are considered to be Class I medical devices and have to be marked with the letters CE or (from 2001) they can be withdrawn from sale. Frames made outside the European single market are exempt, hence the bare inner sides of such brands as RVS by V from Turkey (p. 171).

clip-over: A form of auxiliary spectacle front, often the means of attaching sun lenses. Other forms include the grab front and the drop front.

combination frame: A frame in which the front is made from more than one material, commonly a mix of a metal and a plastic, such as »acetate. Combination frames were particularly popular for men in the 1950s and 1960s.

curl sides: C-shaped »sides that loop around the ears, believed to have been promoted first at London's Great Exhibition of 1851; sometimes known in the United States as riding bows. Historically, many industrial protection goggles had curl sides.

end [3]: The term used for the terminal piece of a spectacle »side, sometimes also known as a tip. Many

Library frame

otherwise metal frames have plastic end covers, sometimes extending well up the side's length.

epoxy resin: A thermosetting (sets permanently when heated) plastic frame material that doesn't require a plasticizer. The best-known example is »Optyl (which is also the name of a manufacturer). Epoxy resin is compression-moulded, which means that frames are very hard and thus scratch-resistant, and it also retains colour well.

extrusion process: A method of producing plain or patterned acetate sheet for spectacle frames by squeezing the raw materials from nozzles and flattening the resulting mixture between rollers. During the 1950s to 1970s this process gradually replaced the old »block method, but was unable to reproduce the latter method's decorative detail.

eyeglasses: Historically a synonym for »'spectacles', the word is now usually reserved for a particular type of folding »eyewear, although it is still applied more generally in North America.

eyewear: Devices worn on the face for the correction of visual error or to provide protection.

front: The front portion of a spectacle frame, incorporating the »rims and »bridge and possibly »lugs, to which the »joints are attached. Fronts may be of the same material as or different from the »sides, and they may have interchangeable decorative trim. »Combination fronts are made of more than one material.

gold: Pure gold (24 carat) is generally too soft to make spectacle frames; 'solid-gold' frames, such as those produced in the 1980s by Neostyle (p. 97), were more likely to be an alloy containing 14- or 18-carat gold. The gold content is normally stamped on the underside of the »bridge in the form of a fraction. Note that the term 'carat gold' used on its own always denotes an alloy. In the United States the word is normally spelled 'karat', and 'carat' has a separate meaning as a fifth of a gram.

Rolled-gold frames (or **gold-filled**, often abbreviated in product catalogues to GF), such as those made by Algha (p. 55) or the French firm Henry Jullien, involve a thin layer of maybe 14-carat gold wrapped around a core of base metal. The frames can rust if the surface of this layer is broken, although the coating is robust and can withstand expansion by heat. From the 1960s **gold plating** became more common, spurred by developments within the jewellery trade, although the gold layer may be very thin and may require additional lacquering for protection. The price of gold quadrupled in 1980 and in consequence many spectacle manufacturers ceased using it.

half-eye spectacles: Spectacles with »rims (or rimless »lenses) that cover only the lower half of the field of view, suitable for wearers who require an optical correction for near vision only and allowing them to peer over the top of the spectacles for distance vision. Since such frames are mainly used for reading or close work, they have less often been produced in fashionable styles.

hinge *see* »joint.

horn rim: A generally meaningless term, since most of the old-fashioned frames described as 'horn-rimmed' were not made of horn. It is possible that some users of the term have assumed, wrongly, that the word related to the shape (as in pointed horns). Horn was, however, a popular frame material, particularly that derived from the European buffalo. It polishes well to produce a hard surface, and there are luxury frame makers who continue with its use.

joint [4]: The proper term for a hinge. Joints may be attached by screws, rivets or pins in a horizontal or vertical setting. Sprung joints were patented by Frederick Buonapart Anderson of Gravesend, Kent, in 1850.

lens [5]: The optical component of »spectacles, secured to the frame traditionally in the form of a glazed »rim, but rimless styles and other forms of lens mounting (including the use of adhesives or nylon stitching) have influenced designs in recent years. Common lens shapes include round, oval, rectangular (oblong), panto-round oval (»PRO), upswept and cat's-eye. Such designs as those of J.F. Rey (p. 157) demonstrate that even when rims are used the lenses no longer need to sit within them.

library frame: A term often applied to a particularly thick plastic frame that gives the wearer a studious look.

lorgnette: Spectacles that are not worn continuously but are supported in front of the face with a handle to the side. Lorgnettes were invented in the late eighteenth century and were popular throughout the nineteenth century.

lug [6]: An extension, usually to the central or upper portion of the »rim, providing housing for a »joint. Lugs can be extended for decorative reasons, or wrapped round to provide a curvaceous style.

marcasite: The name of this mineral (iron sulphide) is used to refer to a form of lustrous pyrite used as a decorative gemstone on spectacle frames, often on the upswept corners of upper »rims in women's spectacle frames of the 1950s. The chemical instability and brittle nature of true marcasite would make it unsuitable for this use. Depending on the quality of the frame, the gems may be set or merely glued.

metal: A class of material used for spectacle frames, preferred by some for its hardness, durability and suppleness, and for its design potential to realize clean lines. Eyewear metals have included »gold, silver, iron, steel, aluminium and »titanium. Various alloys, such as »Monel, have also been used. Metal frames have occasionally fallen out of favour but have consistently come back into fashion, although they can get hot in the sun. Metal spectacle frames can be constructed from metal wire, or moulded. Patterns can be cut, stamped, engraved or dissolved with acid (etched).

Monel: An extremely strong and resilient metal alloy consisting of up to 70 per cent nickel and at least 25 per cent copper, and a derivative of »nickel silver. Its hardness has made it more suited to spectacle »fronts than to other component parts, and it was used notably for American Optical's Numont rimless mounting in the late 1940s (see p. 23).

monocle: A form of corrective eyewear comprising a single »lens. Although usually round, monocles can be almost any shape that will fit comfortably within the bone structure of the orbit (eye socket). They may be either rimmed or rimless, and may have a small handle or loop for a suspension cord. Galleried monocles (with an edge-like extension to the rim) offer a more secure fit, and small monocular devices with longer handles (manocles) are sometimes classified alongside them by historians of eyewear and visual aids.

NHS spectacles: Frames approved for supply under the British National Health Service, free to all from the NHS's foundation in 1948 and then, from 1951 until the mid-1980s, free or subsidized to certain qualifying groups. Such frames usually have an NH mark on them, plus a further letter code for the manufacturer.

nickel silver: A very popular metal frame material used in preference to steel and known historically as German silver. It contains no silver at all and usually comprises at least 60 per cent copper plus varying amounts of nickel and smaller quantities of zinc. »Monel was a derivative. Nickel silver frames have often been plated with pure nickel after manufacture. Nickel in its pure form is a well-known allergen and would fall foul of the European Nickel Directive and international standards introduced in 1998.

nitrate: A popular plastic frame material in the first half of the twentieth century. Nitrate frames reacted with human sweat to produce nitric acid, which could cause skin irritation; they were also inflammable, although the risk of combustion was largely confined to the optician's workbench during frame adjustment. They were considered to keep their shape well, even in hot and humid conditions (such as those found in parts of America), but on account of the material's inherent instability most historic examples have now disintegrated.

nylon: One early use of this synthetic polymer, or polyamide (first produced in the mid-1930s), was as a virtually unbreakable plastic frame material, employed in particular in the form of a cord to support the lenses in a semi-rimless »supra frame. Moulded nylon frames are also made, but expense dictates that these are suitable only for large production runs, hence nylon being more usually encountered in popular models of sunglasses. Properly transparent polyamides, the equal of »acetate, have been in use since the early 1990s. Early nylons were very allergenic, but modern polyamides have largely rectified this problem. SPX, introduced by Silhouette (p. 103) in 1982, was the first super-polyamide frame material to overcome the problem of atmospheric water absorption.

Optyl: An »epoxy resin frame material launched officially in 1968. Although of similar density to most other plastics, Optyl frames require no metal reinforcement, allowing the finished product to be lighter.

pad [7]: The part of a frame pressing against the nose. It may be integral to the »rim (although often not sharing its colour), or made from a different material and attached to the inner rims or suspended from the mounting of the »bridge.

Perspex: A well-known trade name for the acrylic resin frame material polymethylmethacrylate (PMMA). Its

PRO frame

most common use was as the main frame material in the »nylon »supra frames of the 1950s and 1960s.

pince-nez: A type of spectacle without »sides, featuring a spring clip or extending bar »bridge, allowing the frame to cling firmly to the nose in a pinching action. Pince-nez were introduced in the late nineteenth century and remained popular for the first half of the twentieth century. Early nose spectacles are not pince-nez, as they generally simply rest on the nose and require support from the hand.

plano: Having no optical prescription. Some people who do not require spectacles have nonetheless worn them for reasons of fashion, glazed with plano lenses.

plastic: A class of material used for spectacle frames, preferred by some for its comfort, fit and soft feel. The first plastics used in eyewear (in the early twentieth century) were usually termed 'imitation shell'. In the 1920s there was increasing use of plastic for individual spectacle components, such as »pads. By the 1950s most frames were plastic, but the fashion battle of plastic versus »metal has swung back

and forth since then. The two most common plastics to have been used for frames are »acetate and »nitrate.

prescription house: An optical laboratory in which finished spectacles are made up to an optical prescription. The frames are often bought in from a manufacturer.

PRO frame: PRO stands for 'panto[scopic]-round-oval', a type of non-round »rim shape introduced in the nineteenth century (as 'pantoscopic' half-eye rims) and revived in the second half of the twentieth century.

progressive lens: A spectacle lens featuring a gradually increasing change in prescription power across its surface, designed for the correction of presbyopia (long-sightedness caused by loss of elasticity of the lens in the eye); also known as a progressive addition lens (PAL) or varifocal lens. The first progressive lens, the Varilux, was produced in 1959 by the French company Essilor.

propionate: A plastic frame material that gained popularity in the 1980s; its use is sometimes denoted on a

frame by the initials CP ('cellulose propionate'). It is lighter and longer-lasting than »acetate, but early propionate could be used only to make moulded frames and so suited only those designs where the decoration could be pre-cast.

reading stone: A lens of hemispherical form that is held flat against the object to be viewed. Reading stones are considered to be the earliest form of practical vision aid. The concept was described in *c*. AD 1000 in the *Book of Optics* by the Arabian scholar Ibn al-Haytham (*c*. 965–*c*. 1040; also known as Alhazen). Reading stones are the ancestors of the modern dome-shaped desk magnifiers.

rim [8]: The part of the frame surrounding the »lens; also known as eye frames. The lens may be lodged in a groove in the inner surface of the rim or otherwise attached by screws, rivets or glued mounts. Various attempts have been made to reduce the extent of rim necessary to secure the lenses, and rimless spectacle styles do away with them altogether. The rims may incorporate the »pads of the »bridge.

side [9]: Spectacle frames have two 'arms' (as they are often referred to in common usage), or sides; in the United States and in historic English they are known as 'temples' or 'temple pieces'. Sides may be reinforced with »metal. So-called 'library' sides are notably thicker. Sides developed from tie-on cords, and there is no hard evidence that sides existed before the 1720s, although sculptural evidence from church fittings and gravestones may indicate their existence prior to a famous trade card (*c*. 1727–30) of Edward Scarlett of Soho, which illustrated spectacles with spiral-ended sides.

spectacles: The preferred term for 'glasses', also known in the United States as 'eyeglasses'. Spectacles may be glazed with prescription lenses for optical use or with »plano tints for use as »sunglasses.

stainless steel: A »metal alloy material used for some rimless spectacle mounts and occasionally for full frames, as exemplified by ic! berlin (p. 161). Stainless-steel frames are light because this strong material can be used in thinner form than other materials.

Windsor frame

sunglasses: A form of spectacles with tinted lenses designed for outdoor use in sunny conditions, but increasingly worn for reasons of fashion in non-sunny conditions, and even indoors. Despite some historic precedents, notably in Venice in the 1780s, it is usually misleading to speak of sunglasses before the twentieth century, and their use was not widespread until the 1920s in the United States and after the Second World War in many European countries.

supra: A type of spectacle mount featuring an upper frame of plastic or metal with a suspended wire or cord supporting the »lens (see, for example, p. 84, no. 3), first produced in the 1940s. The perceived advantage was that only half a frame was necessary, thereby reducing the conspicuousness of the frame to the onlooker, although in due course the remaining section of »rim became one of the more decorative and hence noticeable frame styles.

The supra was invented and patented in Britain in 1939 by Neville Chappell, but he was prevented by war service from exploiting his invention straight away. During the war London optometrist Hyman (Harry) Freeman came up with an identical solution, unaware of the prior patent until he tried to protect his own invention. He suggested the use of »nylon for the cord in 1946.

The first supras were the 'browline' »combination frames, using metal bands as support for the lenses, produced from about 1947 by Shuron in the United States. The French Nylor frames, utilizing nylon cord for support, were produced by the Société des Lunetiers, also under licence from Chappell, from 1954. Supras are very easy to glaze because the lenses can simply be sprung in.

Swarovski stones: A widely known brand name for a form of cut crystal stone from the Austrian Tyrol, used by many frame manufacturers to decorate »fronts, »sides and »ends. The company was founded by Daniel Swarovski in 1895.

Various chemical coatings on the stones permit the refraction of light in brilliant colours. The shimmering 'aurora borealis' effect was developed in 1956 in collaboration with Christian Dior. Since the mid-1970s it has been possible to 'hot fix' the stones to a wide range of materials. The Swarovski name is now used separately as a designer fashion brand, and a range of Swarovski Eyewear has been produced under licence by Silhouette (p. 103) and, more recently, by the Italian Marcolin Group. In 2008 American Jamal Robinson claimed to be the first designer to place Swarovski stones directly on to the lenses of sunglasses, later producing bespoke frames for rap artists Sean Booth and Soulja Boy, among others; since 2010 he has made the concept commercially available via his company Desiar Eyewear.

temple/temple piece: *see* »side.

titanium: An ultra-lightweight »metal that is also inert and does not react with human tissue. Spectacle frames made of titanium were introduced in the 1980s.

tortoiseshell: The first (natural) material with plastic properties to be used to make frames. More accurately it is turtleshell, derived from the flexible outer carapace of the hawksbill turtle. Real shell can be highly polished and quite transparent if thin enough. The best examples produce a brown/yellow mottled effect; blond or amber shell frames are even more exclusive, owing to the small number of suitable plates in any one carapace.

The hawksbill turtle has been a protected species since 1970 and international trade of the species is prohibited. This has led to an explosion in »acetate materials imitative of real shell. Early twentieth-century materials were known by various brand names, including 'imshell', but many modern manufacturers simply use the word 'shell' to describe a frame by its visual appearance rather than its material composition.

Windsor frame: A classic style of the 1920s–40s, comprising (normally) a round metal eye shape with plastic-covered »rims but exposed »bridge and »joints. A form of Windsor frame was patented by American Optical (p. 23) in 1917.

Xylonite: A versatile though flammable plastic from the family of cellulose »acetates, used in frame making from around the 1920s. It could be supplied in sheet stock, either in colours or as a mottled imitation shell. The latter style was often used as »rim covers on round »Windsor frames. The American word Zylonite is used to denote a wider range of commercially produced acetate materials.

Further Reading

Albarello, A., and Veronese, M., *Stories of Looks and Visions: Galleria Guglielmo Tabacchi*, Turin (Umberto Allemandi) 2009

Alberoni, F., *Occhiali Italiani*, Italy (ANFAO) 1986

Andressen, B.M., *Spectacles: From Utility Article to Cult Object*, Stuttgart (Arnoldsche Art Publishers) 1998

Bronson, L.D., *Early American Specs: An Exciting Collectible*, Glendale, Calif. (Occidental Publishing Company) 1974

Bruneni, J. L., *Looking Back: An Illustrated History of the American Ophthalmic Industry*, Torrance, Calif. (Optical Laboratories Association) 1994

Corson, R., *Fashions in Eyeglasses*, London (Peter Owen) 1980

Crestin-Billet, F., *Collectable Eyeglasses*, Paris (Flammarion); London (Thames & Hudson) 2004

Cutler and Gross, *Forty Years of Vision and Style 1969–2009*, London (Cutler and Gross) 2009

Dowaliby, M., *Modern Eyewear: Fashion and Cosmetic Dispensing*, Chicago (The Professional Press) 1961

Gelius, S., von Kuon, E., Pellert H., Rodenstock, R., and Zwack, H., *Rodenstock 100 Years for Better Vision*, Munich (Optische Werke G. Rodenstock) 1977

Goldoni, L., *A Far-Sighted Man: Luxottica 1961–1991*, Treviso (Gruppo Luxottica) 1991

Gottschling, H., Haffmans, D., Haffmans, P., and Krueger, M. (eds), *Five Years Mykita*, Berlin (Mykita GmbH) 2008

Gross, K.J., Stone, J., and Solomon, M., *Spectacles*, London (Thames & Hudson) 1994

Handley, N., 'Some Ever-Present Themes in Spectacle Frame Design', *Optometry in Practice* 5 (2004), pp. 85–98

Jockel, N., *Vor Augen: Formen, Geschichte und Wirkungen der Brille*, Hamburg (Museum für Kunst und Gewerbe) 1986

Lotto, E. De, *From Nero's Emerald to the Cadore Glasses*, Pieve di Cadore, Italy (Tiziano Printing House) 1956 (4th edn, 2000)

Marly, P., *Spectacles and Spyglasses*, Paris (Editions Hoebeke) 1988

Rosenthal, J.W., *Spectacles and Other Vision Aids: A History and Guide to Collecting*, San Francisco (Norman Publishing) 1996

Rossi, F., *Brillen: Vom Leseglas zum modischen Accessoire*, Munich (Callwey) 1989

Schiffer, N., *Eyeglass Retrospective: Where Fashion Meets Science*, Atglen, Penn. (Schiffer Publishing) 2000

Shabazz, J., *Back in the Days*, New York (PowerHouse) 2001

Where to See Cult Eyewear

UNITED KINGDOM

British Optical Association Museum, College of
Optometrists, 42 Craven Street, London WC2N 5NG;
college-optometrists.org/museum

Victoria and Albert Museum, Cromwell Road,
London SW7 2RL;
vam.ac.uk

UNITED STATES

Museum of Vision, Foundation of the
American Academy of Ophthalmology,
655 Beach Street, San Francisco, CA 94109;
museumofvision.org

CANADA

Museum of Vision Science, School of Optometry,
University of Waterloo, Ontario N2L 3G1;
optometry.uwaterloo.ca/museum

FRANCE

Viséum – Musée de la Lunette,
Place Jean-Jaurès, 39400 Morez;
morez1900.net/Viseum.htm

GERMANY

Optisches Museum der Ernst-Abbe-Stiftung,
Carl-Zeiss-Platz, D07753 Jena;
optischesmuseum.de

ITALY

Il Museo dell'Occhiale, via Arsenale 15,
32044 Pieve di Cadore, Belluno;
museodellocchiale.it

THE NETHERLANDS

Stichting Nationaal Brilmuseum,
Gasthuismolensteeg 7, 1016 AM, Amsterdam;
brilmuseumamsterdam.nl

Picture Credits

STEPHEN ADNITT: 31

ALAIN MIKLI INTERNATIONAL: 92; 93; 94t–b; 95b; 134; 135; 136 (all); 137.5; 137.6

AMERICAN OPTICAL HERITAGE MUSEUM: 22; 24br; 25.2 and .3

MARTIN BRONSON: 107b

CARTIER: 35t and b (N. Welsh, Collection Cartier); 35c; 36tl and tr; 36cb (Studio Triple V); 36b (Katel Riou); 37tl and tr; 37c (A. Garreau); 37b (Studio Triple V)

CAT'S COLLECTION/CORBIS: 44

ALEXANDRE COCO: 114tl, tc, tr, ct and cb

THE COLLEGE OF OPTOMETRISTS: 6; 8b (Derek Moore); 12t (Derek Moore); 13tr; 20.2 and .5; 21.2; 23t; 24t; 25.1; 26 (with permission); 27.1; 47t and ct; 54; 57.3; 63b; 67t and b; 68tl and tr (UK Optical Archive); 70; 71.1 (UK Optical Archive); 76 (with permission of Rodenstock); 78t (with permission of Rodenstock); 80tl and b (with permission of Rodenstock); 82; 83t and b; 84.1; 84.2; 85tl and tr; 86; 87b; 88b; 89cb

THE COLLEGE OF OPTOMETRISTS/ELLIOTT FRANKS: 2; 4c and b; 5t–b; 7; 8t; 9tl, tr and b; 10t and b; 11.1, .3 and .4; 13t, ct and cb; 14t, cb and 14b; 15t (courtesy of Roger Pope & Partners) and b; 16t–b; 17b; 20t; 23b; 24bl; 25.4 and .5; 27.2 and .4 (courtesy of Lawrence Jenkin); 28t and cb (courtesy of Gordon Turner); 28ct and b; 29.1, .4 and .6 (courtesy of Gordon Turner); 29.2, .3, and .5; 30t and c; 30b (courtesy of Lawrence Jenkin); 32t, ct and cb; 32b (courtesy of Lawrence Jenkin); 33t and b; 33ct and cb (courtesy of Lawrence Jenkin); 36ct; 40t–b; 46ct, cb and b (courtesy of Lawrence Jenkin); 47cb; 47b (courtesy of Lawrence Jenkin); 50.4 (courtesy of Oliver Goldsmith); 50.5 and .6; 51.4 (courtesy of Gordon Turner); 52.1–5 (courtesy of Oliver Goldsmith); 53 (with permission of Imperial Tobacco Limited); 56t–b; 57.1, .2, .4, and .5; 58t–b; 59t–b; 60r; 64c and b; 65t–b; 68c and b; 71.3 and .5; 75l; 77b; 78ct and cb (courtesy of Arckiv); 79ct and b (courtesy of Roger Pope & Partners); 80r; 81t and b (courtesy of Arckiv); 84.3–6; 85ct, cb and b; 88cb; 89t; 91t (courtesy of Lawrence Jenkin); 91c and b; 95t and c; 97t l–b; 98t–b; 99t–b; 100t–b; 104ct and b; 106.1–3; 107t; 108 (courtesy of Lawrence Jenkin); 109t and b (courtesy of Lawrence Jenkin); 109c; 110t (courtesy of Lawrence Jenkin); 110ct, cb and b; 111t–b; 114b; 115.4; 121t and c; 122t; 123; 125tl and c; 126t–b; 127ct and b; 132t; 133bl (courtesy of Arckiv); 137.1–4 (courtesy of Gordon Turner); 158t; 158c (courtesy of Roger Pope & Partners); 167t; 168cb and b; 169t; 171c and b; 172t and b; 173t and b; 176t; 179t, ctr and b; 180; 181l and r; 182; 184; 185

COLUMBIA PICTURES/THE RONALD GRANT ARCHIVE: 69

CUTLER AND GROSS: 112 (photo by: Luis Montero; model: Eloise; art direction: Monica Chong); 114.1; 115.2; 115.3 (photo by: Luis Montero; model: Marco; art direction: Monica Chong)

C.W. DIXEY & SON: 19t and b; 20.3, .4 and .6; 21.1 .3 and .4

DE RIGO VISION: 144; 145 (all); 146; 147t–b; 148.1–4; 149

MARGARET DOWALIBY: 75r

VIDAL ERKOHEN: 45t–b; 46t; 67c

FEDERATION OF MANUFACTURING OPTICIANS: 55b; 79t; 178c and b; 179cb

HANS FIEBIG/HANS CUSTOM OPTIK, INC./JIM BELCHER: 101 (all)

ELLIOTT FRANKS: 117

NEIL HANDLEY: 11.2 (courtesy Weismüller Collection); 12b (courtesy Weismüller Collection); 13b; 14ct; 55t; 60r; 71.2 and .4; 106.4 (courtesy Weismüller Collection); 115.1 (courtesy of Weismüller Collection); 129.4

DAVE HOGAN/GETTY IMAGES: 113

IC BERLIN! BRILLEN GMBH: 160; 161t–b; 162t–b; 163t–b; 164t–b; 165t and b

LAWRENCE JENKIN: 27.3

J.F. REY EYEWEAR DESIGN/CASECO LTD: 156; 157t and b; 158b; 159t–b

KIRK ORIGINALS: 38; 39; 41t and b; 42.1–4; 43t–b

L.A. EYEWORKS: 4t; 138; 139t–b; 140 (all); 141t–b; 142t–b; 143t, cb and b

O. PH. L – LAFONT: 118; 119 (all); 120t and b; 121b; 122ct, cb and b

HAYWOOD MAGEE/PICTURE POST/HULTON ARCHIVE/GETTY IMAGES: 18

GUY MARÉ: 78b; 79cb

MYKITA GMBH: 166; 167c and b; 168t and ct; 169c and b

NEOSTYLE GMBH & VO KG: 96; 97tr

OLIVER GOLDSMITH: 48; 49t and b; 50.1–3; 51.1–3

OP COUTURE BRILLEN GMBH/CAZAL: 130; 131t and b; 132b; 133t and c; 133br

PIERRE MARLY: 72; 73l and r; 74t–b

POLAROID/POLAROID UK LTD: 62; 63t; 64tl and tr

ROBERT LA ROCHE: 124; 125tr and b; 127t and cb; 128.1–7; 129.1–3 and .5

RVS BY V: 170; 171t; 173c

SERGE KIRCHHOFER ARCHIVE (COURTESY OF WESTLICHT PHOTOGRAPHICA AUCTION/PETER COELN GMBH): 77t; 87t; 88t and ct; 89ctl, ctr and b; 90t–b

SILHOUETTE INTERNATIONAL SCHMIED AG: 17t; 102; 103.1–5; 104 t and cb; 105t–b; 106.5

SILMO: 178t

STARTRACKS PHOTO/REX FEATURES: 34

TD TOM DAVIES LTD: jacket, front; 174; 175; 176c and b; 177t–b; 179ctl

THEO BVBA: jacket, back; 150; 151t–b; 152.1–4; 153.1–4; 154 (all); 155t and b

PENNY TWEEDIE/CORBIS: 61

UNIVERSAL/THE KOBAL COLLECTION: 66

Index

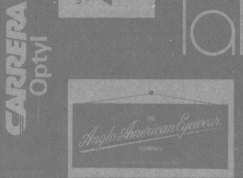